Credits

Author
John P. Doran

Reviewers
Edward Davies
Richard Moore
H. Woodman

Acquisition Editor
Erol Staveley

Lead Technical Editor
Azharuddin Sheikh

Technical Editor
Hardik Soni

Copy Editors
Alfida Paiva
Aditya Nair
Insiya Morbiwala

Project Coordinator
Anugya Khurana

Proofreader
Martin Diver

Indexers
Hemangini Bari
Tejal R. Soni

Production Coordinator
Arvindkumar Gupta

Cover Work
Arvindkumar Gupta

About the Author

John P. Doran is a technical game designer who has been creating games for over 10 years. He has worked on an assortment of games in teams from just himself to over 70 in-student, mod, indie, and professional projects.

He previously worked at LucasArts on *Star Wars: 1313* as a Game Design Intern. He was the only junior designer in a team of seniors. He later graduated from DigiPen Institute of Technology in Redmond, WA with a Bachelor of Science degree in Game Design.

John is currently a Software Engineer at DigiPen's Singapore campus, where he tutors students and assists them with difficulties in Computer Science concepts, programming, linear algebra, game design, and advanced usage of UDK, Flash, and Unity in a development environment.

This is his second book; previously he was coauthor for the book *UDK iOS Game Development Beginner's Guide, Packt Publishing.*

He can be found online at http://johnpdoran.com and can be contacted at john@johnpdoran.com.

Mastering UDK
Gam
HOT

Eight proj   he
Unreal De

John P. Do

PUBLISHING

BIRMINGHAM - MUMBAI

Mastering UDK Game Development
HOTSH⊕T

First published: March 2013

Production Reference: 1080313

Published by Packt Publishing Ltd.
Livery Place
35 Livery Street
Birmingham B3 2PB, UK.

ISBN 978-1-84969-560-2

www.packtpub.com

Cover Image by John P. Doran (john@johnpdoran.com)

Acknowledgement

A big thanks goes to my good friends, James King, who provided the three-dimensional ship models used in *Project 2, Terror in Deep Space*, and Helen Rachael Morris, for giving me the HUD and inventory images. They make their respective projects look so much better, and I couldn't have done it without them.

I want to thank my brother Chris Doran and my girlfriend Hannah Mai for being supportive and patient with me as I spent my free time and weekends away from them to finish this book.

On that same note, I also want to thank Samir Abou Samra and Elie Hosry for their support and encouragement while I was working on this book, as well as the rest of the DigiPen Singapore staff.

Thanks to Erol Staveley who approached me about writing again, as well as everyone else at Packt Publishing who were so helpful, as always!

Last but not least, I'd like to thank my family as well as my parents, Joseph and Sandra Doran, who took me seriously when I told them I wanted to make games for living.

About the Reviewers

Edward Davies has a BA in Game Art and Animation from the University of Glamorgan. He is currently pursuing an MA in Animation, with which he will graduate in 2013.

He has a great interest in concept art and game development with the Unreal (UDK) Games Engine.

Find out more about Edward's work at the following links:

- ▶ **DeviantArt** – http://kungfoowiz.deviantart.com
- ▶ **Website** – http://kungfoowiz.weebly.com
- ▶ **Blog** – http://kungfoowiz.blogspot.com

Richard Moore graduated in 2009, studying video game design at Hull School of Art and Design (University of Lincoln), where he first began expanding his creativity by working as a freelance designer in Hull, East Yorkshire and in London. He has worked on a number of different projects, such as a collection of stylish websites, logos, brochures, business cards, web banners, animated graphics, and e-mail marketing campaigns, with clients from different industry backgrounds.

Through the clouds lies his passion in video game development and the complete creation of three-dimensional art, including modeling, texturing, and high-resolution rendering. He does game documentation and conceptual drawings as well. He will always take any opportunity to meet as many different people from the game-development community, and as a result, he has attended the Game Grads career fair and participated in the Game Republic 2009 student showcase in Sheffield and Platform 2010, Hull's first Digital and Gaming event, where he won the award for best character design.

In March 2011, he participated in Platform Expo 2011, Hull's second video game expedition, where he entered the video game showcase for the second consecutive year and won the second prize for his outstanding contribution to video game design. In July 2011, he volunteered as a marketing assistant/designer for an online-based video games magazine where he created a brand new look and feel for the magazine. He also dazzled with written reviews on the latest video game titles, and talking to clients about potential advertising coverage within the magazine and online, not to mention designing a new weekly newsletter and PR website.

In September 2011, he wrote his first published book, *Unreal Development Kit Beginner's Guide*, which teaches the fundamentals of level design and how to implement level design, lighting, environmental effects, movement, terrain, map creation, item placement, kismet, materials, and complex event sequences using the Unreal Engine. He was also a technical reviewer for another published book, *Unreal Development Kit iOS Development*, which serves as an introduction to mobile gaming deployment on iOS devices. He is currently reviewing two new books dedicated to UDK that are due out in 2013.

As a result, he is now working as a Graphic Artist / iPad Technician for an award-winning company based in Central London that thrives on technology and creates ground-breaking iPad apps, high-impact short films, and bespoke video games. In his spare time, he focuses more on freelance design and development work with up-and-coming companies and he loves to ramble on about video game news. In 2013, he plans to start his very own video game podcast where he will continue to ramble on about the latest news from the gaming world and review and preview titles, and much more.

Hamish Woodman has studied landscape architecture and teaches high school Art and Technology at Victoria University of Wellington. He is currently the art-and-design half of fledgling game-development company Broken Planet with code wizard Stephen Townshend; they are working (in their spare time around work and family) on producing a title for Steam using the UDK, and they blog about their learning and progress at `http://brokenplanet.co.nz/blog/` to help others attempt similar projects.

www.PacktPub.com

Support files, eBooks, discount offers and more

You might want to visit www.PacktPub.com for support files and downloads related to your book.

Did you know that Packt offers eBook versions of every book published, with PDF and ePub files available? You can upgrade to the eBook version at www.PacktPub.com and as a print book customer, you are entitled to a discount on the eBook copy. Get in touch with us at service@packtpub.com for more details.

At www.PacktPub.com, you can also read a collection of free technical articles, sign up for a range of free newsletters and receive exclusive discounts and offers on Packt books and eBooks.

http://PacktLib.PacktPub.com

Do you need instant solutions to your IT questions? PacktLib is Packt's online digital book library. Here, you can access, read and search across Packt's entire library of books.

Why Subscribe?
- Fully searchable across every book published by Packt
- Copy and paste, print and bookmark content
- On demand and accessible via web browser

Free Access for Packt account holders

If you have an account with Packt at www.PacktPub.com, you can use this to access PacktLib today and view nine entirely free books. Simply use your login credentials for immediate access.

Table of Contents

Preface

The Unreal Development Kit (UDK) is the free version of the popular and award-winning Unreal Engine 3. A truly powerful tool for game development, there has never been a better time to use it for both commercial and independent projects.

Mastering UDK Game Development Hotshot takes a clear, step-by-step approach to building a series of game projects using the Unreal Development Kit. By using this book, you will be able to create a two-dimensional-style platformer, a rail-shooter spaceship, as well your very own custom HUD. We then move on to more advanced projects, such as the creation of an inventory system for a Western RPG, complete with dynamic objects that can be dropped anywhere in the game world. On top of all of this, you'll also learn how to quickly and efficiently create modular environments within the UDK itself.

You'll discover how you can exploit the UDK to the fullest extent, making it possible to create a series of exciting projects within the UDK. We will also use the popular industry tool Scaleform in Flash to create user experiences. Finally, we will also go over how to get started in UnrealScript. By learning about advanced functionality via engaging practical examples, you too can take your game to the next level and stand out from the crowd.

What this book covers

Project 1, Advanced Kismet – Creating a Third-person Platformer, starts by creating a side-scrolling platformer game using the three-dimensional engine to create two-dimensional gameplay. In this project, the player can move left and right, jump on static and moving platforms, and collect coins/collectables, some of which may modify the player's behavior.

Project 2, Terror in Deep Space, will have us creating a three-dimensional rail-shooter game where the player controls a ship. This ship can move around the screen and shoot projectiles out. Enemies and obstacles will spawn towards the player and the player will avoid/shoot them.

Project 3, Terror in Deep Space 2: Even Deeper, will have us continuing along the same path as the previous project. We will use the basis of the project created in *Project 2, Terror in Deep Space*, and expand upon it by adding enemies that shoot as well as a multitude of asteroids for the player to avoid and/or shoot. We will also add additional functionality, which can be added to practically any game to add polish, such as a HUD, opening cutscene, and the Game Over state.

Project 4, Creating a Custom HUD, will guide us in creating a HUD that can be used within a Medieval RPG and will fit nicely into the provided Epic Citadel map making use of Scaleform and ActionScript 3.0 using Adobe Flash CS6.

Project 5, Creating Environments, will focus on building environments by creating a small, fairly polished map. We will be using the map that we create in this project in the next mission, where we create a fully functional inventory system!

Project 6, Dynamic Loot, will have us creating a dynamic object the player may alter at runtime in order to pick it up or drop it elsewhere, making use of rigid-body physics, or toggle the player's ability to hold it in his hand as he traverses the game environment.

Project 7, Managing Loot, will focus on creating a custom inventory system, making use of a lot of neat features Flash has that should be able to help us in this project. I'll also provide tips and tools that you can use in your own projects. This inventory system will allow us to pick up multiple objects and either equip players with them or drop them on the ground.

Project 8, UnrealScript: A Primer, will have us first gain an understanding on when to use UnrealScript for projects. We will then set up some tools to help us gain an understanding of the code that Epic provided and give some guidance on how object-oriented programming works. After that, we will learn about and install the IDE and write a simple "Hello world!" object. After that we will move on to create another more complicated object with a dynamically flickering light!

What you need for this book

In order to use this book, you need to have a computer with Windows that is capable of running the UDK. It requires a computer with the following system configuration, which are also the minimum requirements for the book:

- ▶ Windows XP SP3 (32-bit only) with DirectX 9.0c
- ▶ 2 GHz or better CPU
- ▶ 2 GB RAM or better
- ▶ A graphics card with Shader Model 3.0 support, such as NVIDIA GeForce 7800

Note that the 64-bit version of Windows 7 is currently the mainstream development environment.

The following configuration is recommended for content development:

► The 64-bit version of Windows 7

► 2.0 GHz or better multicore processor

► 8 GB system RAM

► NVIDIA 8000 series or higher graphics card

Plenty of HDD space is also a must. The UDK will install .NET Framework 3.5 Service Pack 1 if you don't already have it, which will require an Internet connection.

Project 4, *Creating a Custom HUD*, and *Project 7*, *Managing Loot*, will have us use Scaleform. Scaleform does not require us to use Adobe Flash, but we will be using the Flash environment to create our UI content. I will be using the latest version, Adobe Flash CS6, but it should be possible to do most of the things in these projects using a previous version. For those who do not have Flash, Adobe offers a free trial of all their software. For more information on that, please visit `www.adobe.com/go/tryflash/`.

Who this book is for

Mastering UDK Game Development Hotshot is designed for people who want to truly take their projects to the next level and explore the advanced features that the UDK has to offer. Those who are familiar with the basics of creating things in the UDK will have an easier time, but each project contains step-by-step explanations, diagrams, screenshots, and downloadable content that should make it possible for someone with no prior experience to develop using the UDK at an accelerated pace.

Conventions

In this book, you will find several headings appearing frequently.

To give clear instructions of how to complete a procedure or task, we use:

Mission Briefing

This section explains what you will build, with a screenshot of the completed project.

Why Is It Awesome?

This section explains why the project is cool, unique, exciting, and interesting. It describes what advantage the project will give you.

Your Hotshot Objectives

This section explains the major tasks required to complete your project.

- ► Task 1
- ► Task 2
- ► Task 3
- ► Task 4, and so on

Mission Checklist

This section explains any prerequisites for the project, such as resources or libraries that need to be downloaded, and so on.

Task 1

This section explains the task that you will perform.

Prepare for Lift Off

This section explains any preliminary work that you may need to do before beginning work on the task.

Engage Thrusters

This section lists the steps required in order to complete the task.

Objective Complete - Mini Debriefing

This section explains how the steps performed in the previous section allow us to complete the task. This section is mandatory.

Classified Intel

The extra information in this section is relevant to the task.

You will also find a number of styles of text that distinguish between different kinds of information. Here are some examples of these styles, and an explanation of their meaning.

Code words in text are shown as follows: "In the file browser, locate the path of your UDK installation and then go into the `Binaries\GFx\CLICK Tools\` folder."

A block of code is set as follows:

```
// Whenever the mouse moves, we call the mousePosition
// function
stage.addEventListener(MouseEvent.MOUSE_MOVE,
mousePosition);

functionmousePosition(event:MouseEvent)
{
  // Set the cursor's position to the mouse's new one.
  cursor.x = mouseX;
  cursor.y = mouseY;
}
```

New terms and **important words** are shown in bold. Words that you see on the screen, in menus or dialog boxes for example, appear in the text like this: "Underneath the **Player Spawned** event, right-click under the **Instigator** output and select **Create New Object Variable**."

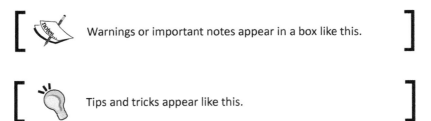

Warnings or important notes appear in a box like this.

Tips and tricks appear like this.

Reader feedback

Feedback from our readers is always welcome. Let us know what you think about this book—what you liked or may have disliked. Reader feedback is important for us to develop titles that you really get the most out of.

To send us general feedback, simply send an e-mail to feedback@packtpub.com, and mention the book title via the subject of your message.

If there is a topic that you have expertise in and you are interested in either writing or contributing to a book, see our author guide on www.packtpub.com/authors.

Customer support

Now that you are the proud owner of a Packt book, we have a number of things to help you to get the most from your purchase.

Downloading the example code

You can download the example code files for all Packt books you have purchased from your account at http://www.packtpub.com. If you purchased this book elsewhere, you can visit http://www.packtpub.com/support and register to have the files e-mailed directly to you.

Downloading the color images of this book

We also provide you a PDF file that has color images of the screenshots/diagrams used in this book. The color images will help you better understand the changes in the output. You can download this file from http://www.packtpub.com/sites/default/files/downloads/5602OT_Mastering_UDK_Game_Development_Color_Graphics.pdf.

Errata

Although we have taken every care to ensure the accuracy of our content, mistakes do happen. If you find a mistake in one of our books—maybe a mistake in the text or the code—we would be grateful if you would report this to us. By doing so, you can save other readers from frustration and help us improve subsequent versions of this book. If you find any errata, please report them by visiting http://www.packtpub.com/submit-errata, selecting your book, clicking on the **errata submission form** link, and entering the details of your errata. Once your errata are verified, your submission will be accepted and the errata will be uploaded on our website, or added to any list of existing errata, under the Errata section of that title. Any existing errata can be viewed by selecting your title from http://www.packtpub.com/support.

Piracy

Piracy of copyright material on the Internet is an ongoing problem across all media. At Packt, we take the protection of our copyright and licenses very seriously. If you come across any illegal copies of our works, in any form, on the Internet, please provide us with the location address or website name immediately so that we can pursue a remedy.

Please contact us at copyright@packtpub.com with a link to the suspected pirated material.

We appreciate your help in protecting our authors, and our ability to bring you valuable content.

Questions

You can contact us at questions@packtpub.com if you are having a problem with any aspect of the book, and we will do our best to address it.

Project 1

Advanced Kismet – Creating a Third-person Platformer

For as long as we have been playing video games, there has been one particular genre that has stayed with us almost from the beginning, the platformer. Starting with *Donkey Kong* with the familiar content that we know, refined in *Super Mario Brothers*, given more action with *Mega Man*, sped up with *Sonic the Hedgehog*, and used even today with games such as *Braid*, *Super Meat Boy*, and *They Bleed Pixels*. There is something that draws us to this specific type of game, especially within the indie game community.

With that in mind, I thought a fitting first project would be to recreate this beloved type of game and prove that UDK is definitely not just for creating first-person shooters.

Mission Briefing

We will be creating a side-scrolling platformer game using the three-dimensional engine to do two-dimensional gameplay. In this project, the player can move left and right, jump on static and moving platforms, and collect coins/collectables, some of which may modify the player's behavior.

We will first approach the project using nothing but Kismet and the UDK Editor. This particular project will be explained with much greater depth than the other projects in order to jog the memory of anyone who has not used UDK in a while and may come up to speed while completing this project.

> For those who need a quick reminder, Kismet is a system of visual scripting in UDK that makes it possible for people to affect the game world and design gameplay events. For teams without a programmer, Kismet can be a godsend. It makes it possible for someone without any coding knowledge to do things that would otherwise require the use of UnrealScript, the programming language that the Unreal engine uses.
>
> In order to create a sequence of events, you will connect a series of **sequential objects** together. This in turn generates a code when the game is run to do the things you want it to do.
>
> In future projects however, I will assume a familiarity with the things I have taught in this project.

Why Is It Awesome?

Once we finish this project, we will have a good understanding of how UDK can be used to create games that it wouldn't necessarily be considered for at first glance; having a three-dimensional engine, we will create a game with two-dimensional gameplay. Also, we will be able to create our very own side-scrolling platformer game in the same vein as *Mario*. We will also learn about some of the assets available in UDK by creating subsequences and prefab objects, which we can apply to future projects.

Your Hotshot Objectives

This project will be split into five tasks. As we are not creating any enemies in our game, we do not have to deal with UnrealScript in this project. It will be a simple systematic process from the beginning to the end. Here is an outline of our tasks:

- ▶ Level and camera creation
- ▶ Adding player functionality
- ▶ Adding platforms
- ▶ Adding collectables/power ups
- ▶ Designing the level layout and background

Mission Checklist

Before we start, let's make sure that we have the latest version of UDK (February 2012 as of this writing), which can be downloaded from `http://www.unrealengine.com/udk/downloads/`.

Apart from that, all of the assets used in this project should already be included within the base UDK installation.

This project and all projects assume that the user has used UDK to some extent in the past and is familiar with the concepts of building brushes as well as navigating around the game environment. The user should also have familiarity with Matinee and know how to do things such as adding keyframes.

That being said, I will do my best to be as descriptive as possible in how to do things.

Level and camera creation

As a start to our project, we will be creating a new level and modifying the camera to create our side-scrolling game.

Prepare for Lift Off

Before we start working on the project, we must first create a new map. To do this, we must first select **File | New Level...** and from the pop up that comes up, select one of the top four options (I selected **Night Lighting**, but it doesn't matter which one you choose).

There are many different options that you can use in determining how UDK is displayed and whether it works for you. I encourage you to take some time to figure out what you like and don't like. While having a Front viewport may be nice, I like having a larger screen space for the **Perspective** view so that I have a better idea what the area I'm creating looks like. This is more my personal preference than anything but it is what I will be using from here on out.

If you wish to follow me, select **View | Viewport Configuration | 1x2 Split** from the top menu so that your screen looks like the following screenshot:

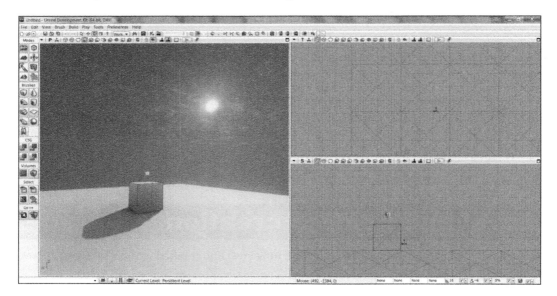

Engage Thrusters

Now that we have a base level to work in, let's start building our game!

1. Bring up the **World Properties** menu by selecting **View | World Properties** from the menu bar at the top of the UDK interface. Type Game Type in the search bar at the top of the **World Properties** menu to bring up the **Game Type** menu and the relevant options for us. From there, change the drop-down menus for both **Default Game Type** and **Game Type for PIE** to **UTDeathmatch**. As we are in the **Zone Info** section, under **Kill Z** set the value to -1000.

2. Now let's make sure our player spawns in the correct position. Select the **PlayerStart_0** object and press *F4* to access the object's Properties window. From there, in the search bar at the top, type Location. Once you find the **Location** vector variable, set the **X** value to 0. Next, type Rotation. Make sure that the **Roll** and **Pitch** options are set to 0 and change the **Yaw** option to 90.

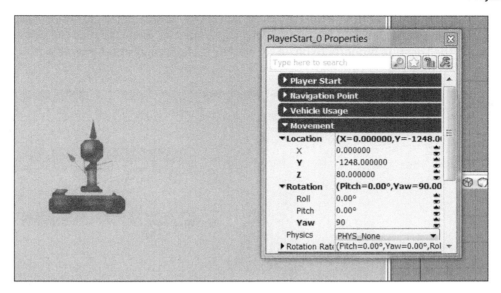

Also, note the numbers listed on the **Y** and **Z** values in the **Location** variable, as we will be using them in a future step.

For those who don't know or who want a reminder, a **variable** is a set of values that are stored in a specific way.

A **vector** in Unreal is a variable (a struct, specifically) that contains three floating point numbers inside it: X, Y, and Z. Conceptually, it corresponds to a three-dimensional Euclidean vector often used in linear algebra; in the previous instance it is used as the position of our **PlayerStart_0** object in three-dimensional space.

3. From here we need to access the **Actors Classes** panel by selecting **View | Browser Windows | Actor Classes**. Inside, click on the **CameraActor** selection that is located under **Categories | Common | CameraActor**.

4. Go back to the editor menu, right-click, and select **Add CameraActor Here**. With the object placed, press *F4* to go to the object's Properties menu. Change the value of **X** in the **Location** property to be -650, and the **Y** and **Z** values to the same position as **PlayerStart_0**, -1248, and 80.

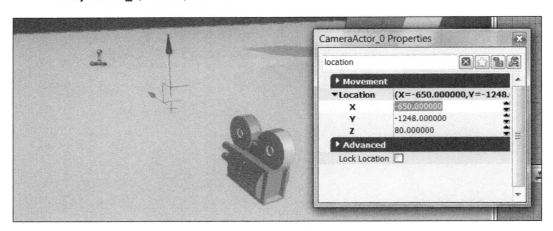

With the necessary objects in place, we open up the Kismet interface by clicking on the **K** icon at the top of the UDK interface on the main toolbar. From there we first need to create a **Player Spawned** event. We then right-click anywhere inside the large area in the upper portion of the interface. Choose to create a **Player Spawned** event by choosing **New Event | Player | Player Spawned** from the menu that pops up. Click on the **Player Spawned** event's **Sequence Event** to have the **Properties** window come up and change the value of **Max Trigger Count** from 1 to 0.

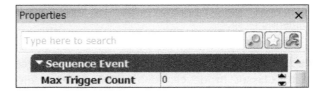

5. Underneath the **Player Spawned** event, right-click under the **Instigator** output and select **Create New Object Variable**. You should see a line connecting the output to the new object variable. If not, click on the connector (the purple triangle) and drag until you select the new variable we created and let go. Click on the new object to open its properties in the bottom-left panel of the Kismet window. Under **Sequence Variable**, we change the value of **Var Name** to Player.

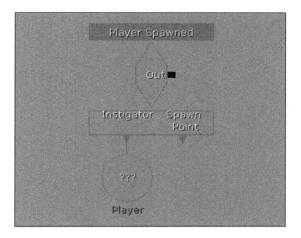

In all the instances where we are using the named variable **Player**, we could use the actual **Player** variable by right-clicking anywhere inside the large area in the upper portion of the interface and selecting **New Variable | Player | Player** and unchecking the **All Players** option in the **Properties** window, but a review of how named variables can be used can be quite useful for things we will be doing in later projects.

6. To the right of the **Player Spawned** event, create a **Set Camera Target** action by right-clicking and selecting **New Action | Camera | Set Camera Target**. Right-click under the **Target** input and select **New Variable | Named Variable**. Click on the variable to open its properties. In **Properties** under **Find Var Name**, type in Player and press *Enter*. You should see the red X change into a green checkmark. Connect the **Player** named variable that we created to the **Target** input.

7. Exit Kismet, click on the **CameraActor_0** actor, and return to Kismet by clicking on the **K** icon on the main toolbar. Right-click on the **Cam Target** input (the pink square) and select **New Object Var With CameraActor_0**. Finally, connect the **Out** output from the **Player Spawned** event to the **In** input from the **Set Camera Target** action we created.

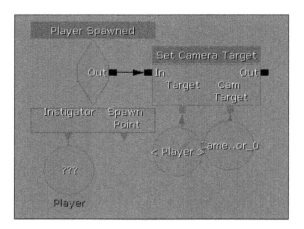

If we started the game at this point, we would notice that when the player spawns we can see the player from a third-person perspective that looks great as long as we do not move. You will notice that the camera does not move with the player and if we move our mouse, our player will turn around and allow us to move in ways that are counter-intuitive to what we are trying to create. Let's fix those issues now.

8. Create an **Attach to Actor** action by right-clicking and selecting **New Action | Actor | Attach to Actor**. Connect the **Target** input to the **Player** variable, and **Attachment** to the **CameraActor_0** variable that we created in the previous section. In the properties for the **Attach to Actor** action, check the **Hard Attach** option and connect the **Out** output from the **Set Camera Target** action to the **In** input of the **Attach to Actor** action.

9. Create a **Toggle Input** action to the right of the **Attach to Actor** action by right-clicking and selecting **New Action | Toggle | Toggle Input**. In the action's properties, uncheck the **Toggle Movement** option and make sure that the **Toggle Turning** option is checked. Connect the **Player** named variable to the **Target** input. Connect the **Out** output of the **Attach to Actor** action to the **Turn Off** input on the **Toggle Input** action.

You can connect all of the targets to the same player, or create multiple **Player** named variables to house all of the things; it makes no difference, but one may make your code look more visually appealing.

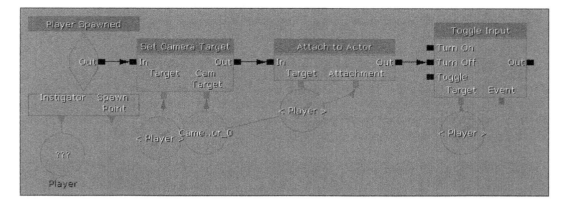

10. Save your project (**File | Save All**) and start your game by pressing *F8* or selecting **Play | In Editor** on the main toolbar.

Objective Complete - Mini Debriefing

We have just created a camera that will follow our player in a similar fashion to that used in side-scroller games. More specifically, we have, through Kismet, told our game that we wish to use a different camera instead of the pawn's default one. We have also disabled the ability for players to turn, for the time being, to prevent nonstandard movement.

Adding player functionality

Now, as amazing as having a camera that follows our player around is, there are still plenty of things that we need to do to get this game to be the best that it can be. For instance, we want the player to move left and right on the screen when we press *A* and *D*. We are also going to adjust the player's jump height and remove the ability to double jump (as it is defaulted in **UTDeathmatch**).

Engage Thrusters

Now, let's get the controls working correctly.

1. With your current level saved, exit out of UDK and open up Windows Explorer. Go to the folder you installed UDK to—that is, to the UDKGame\Config folder. Right-click on the DefaultInput.ini file and select **Copy**. Then use *Ctrl + V* to paste a copy of the file into your folder.

Always create backups of files before you modify them, just in case. On the same note, other projects will assume you are using the default version of this file, so be sure to change the file back when you are ready to move on.

It is often a good practice to have a separate and clean install of UDK for each project you are working on, which acts as a control so that you always know what was there originally.

Alternatively, you can make use of a version control software, like Perforce to enable you to backtrack your steps, but that's beyond the scope of this book.

2. Open the file and replace the following lines:

```
.Bindings=(Name="GBA_MoveForward",Command="Axis aBaseY Speed=1.0")
.Bindings=(Name="GBA_Backward",Command="Axis aBaseY Speed=-1.0")
.Bindings=(Name="GBA_StrafeLeft",Command="Axis aStrafe
Speed=-1.0")
.Bindings=(Name="GBA_StrafeRight",Command="Axis aStrafe
Speed=+1.0")
```

With the following:

```
;-----------------------------------------------------------------
; Hotshot - Begin Changes
;-----------------------------------------------------------------
.Bindings=(Name="GBA_MoveForward",Command="Jump | Axis aUp
Speed=+1.0 AbsoluteAxis=100");
.Bindings=(Name="GBA_StrafeLeft",Command="Axis aBaseY Speed=-1.0")
.Bindings=(Name="GBA_StrafeRight",Command="Axis aBaseY
Speed=+1.0")
;-----------------------------------------------------------------
; Hotshot - End Changes
;-----------------------------------------------------------------
```

Then replace:

```
.Bindings=(Name="Left",Command="GBA_TurnLeft")
.Bindings=(Name="Right",Command="GBA_TurnRight")
```

With:

```
;-----------------------------------------------------------------
; Hotshot - Begin Changes
;-----------------------------------------------------------------
.Bindings=(Name="Left",Command="GBA_StrafeLeft")
.Bindings=(Name="Right",Command="GBA_StrafeRight")
;-----------------------------------------------------------------
; Hotshot - End Changes
;-----------------------------------------------------------------
```

Save the file, and start up the UDK Editor once again.

3. Open up the Kismet Editor. Create a **Console Command** action by right-clicking and choosing **New Action | Misc | Console Command** from the menus.

4. Inside the Properties window type SetJumpZ 750 as the value for **Commands[0]**. Connect the **Player** variable to **Target**. Connect the **Out** output from the **Toggle Input** action to the **In** input of the **Console Command** action.

5. Next, create a **Modify Property** action by right-clicking and choosing **New Action | Object Property | Modify Property** from the menus. Expand **Properties[0]** by clicking on the **+** icon in order to create a new array entry. In the **Property Name** variable, type `MaxMultiJump`. Check the **Modify Property** option and change the value of **Property Value** to `0`. Connect the **Player** variable to the **Target** input. Connect the **Out** output from the **Console Command** action to the **In** input of the **Modify Property** action.

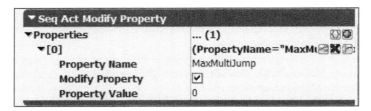

6. Create a **Toggle Cinematic Mode** action by right-clicking beside the **Modify Property** action and selecting **New Action | Toggle | Toggle Cinematic Mode**. Uncheck all of the options apart from the **Hide HUD** option. Connect a **Player** variable to the **Target** input, then the **Out** output from the **Modify Property** action to the **Enable** input of the **Toggle Cinematic Mode** action.

7. Finally, create a **Give Inventory** action by right-clicking and selecting **New Action | Pawn | Give Inventory**. Check the **Clear Existing** and **Force Replace** options. Connect a **Player** variable to the **Target** input, then connect the **Out** output from the **Toggle Cinematic Mode** option to the **In** input of the **Give Inventory** action.

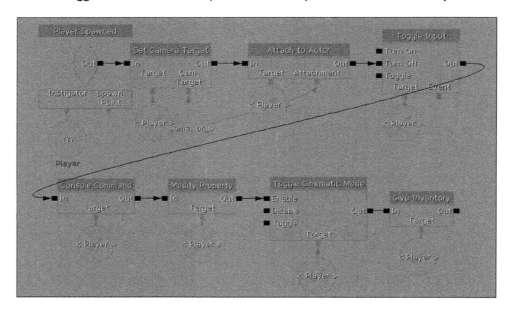

8. Save your project (**File | Save All**) and start your game by pressing *F8* or selecting **Play | In Editor** on the main toolbar.

Objective Complete - Mini Debriefing

With a minimal amount of work, we have accomplished a large amount of what is needed in order to create our side-scrolling platformer game with a player that is controlled similarly to the games we mentioned at the beginning of the project. The player can now move appropriately, and can only jump once. We have removed the player's weapon, and removed the default HUD, and are well on our way to having an awesome project completed!

Classified Intel

To get a clear picture of why/how the changes in our .ini file were made, I feel it is important for me to describe it in detail. The pawn that we are using uses its rotation in determining where it should move by default when we press *W*, the up arrow, or forward on an Xbox 360 controller; the player will move by default straight forward just as you press the down arrow or *S*, or the back arrow/button will move the player backwards. Left and right will either rotate or move the player to the pawn's left or right respectively. Without using UnrealScript to modify the `PlayerController` class and/or pawn, we can just change what the actions do.

Thinking in two-dimensional terms, we want to move the pawn forward when we press the right arrow, move him backwards when our player presses the left arrow, and have the player jump when they press the up arrow or jump.

 Note that the changes that we made to the .ini file were just modifying what the actions associated with the buttons were meant to do. If you wanted to replace the names of the bindings to be associated with their new connections, that is also a viable option; however, it would require replacing a lot more than we already have.

Platforms? In a platformer?

Now that we have the camera system and a functioning player, it would be a good time to start adding things that the player can actually travel to. In this section, we will be creating both static and moving platforms.

Engage Thrusters

That being said, let's add in those platforms!

1. Open the **Content Browser** window in **View | Browser Windows | Content Browser**. Find the following static mesh: `StaticMesh'FoliageDemo.Mesh.S_PavingBlocks_01'`. Click on it and return to the editor's screen. Right-click on the ground of your level and add the mesh to your level (you may need to load it in first) by selecting **Add Static Mesh: FoliageDemo.Mesh.S_PavingBlocks_01**.

2. Delete the static mesh of the box that is currently in the level by clicking on it and pressing the *Delete* key. Select our new platform and change its location to 0, 0, 240 in the same way that we did in the first step. Duplicate the mesh three times and rotate it to face the three sides the camera can see. You can duplicate the object by either holding down *Alt* and dragging or by going to **Edit | Duplicate**. In order to rotate, you can use the translate tool or alter the properties.

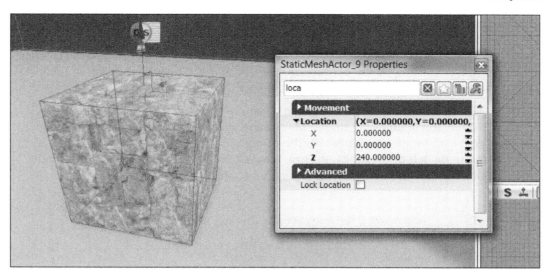

3. Make another duplicate of the top platform by holding *Alt* and dragging along the y axis (256 units). Right-click on the newly created platform and select **Convert | Convert StaticMeshActor To Mover**. Inside the Properties window, change the **Collision Type** to **COLLIDE_BlockAll** and check **Block Rigid Body**.

 You can check the distance from one point to another by holding down your middle mouse button and dragging to where you want to check. This can be quite helpful in games where the spacing between objects matters, which it does quite a lot in a platformer.

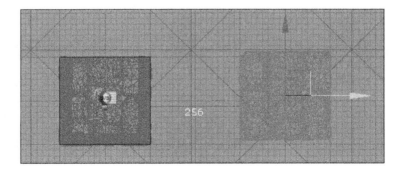

4. Back in Kismet, create a new subsequence by right-clicking and selecting **Create New Sequence : 0 Objs**. When the naming dialog comes up, type in Moving_ Platform_LR for the **Sequence Name** field and click on **OK**. Double-click on the sequence in order to enter it.

5. Create a **Level Loaded** event by right-clicking and selecting **New Event | Level Loaded**. To the right of it create a new Matinee sequence by right-clicking and picking **New Matinee**. Connect the **Loaded and Visible** output of the **Level Loaded** event to the **Play** action of **Matinee**. In the Matinee's properties under **Seq Act Interp**, check **Looping** and **Rewind if Already Playing**.

6. Outside the editor, click on the soon-to-be-moving platform and then go back to Kismet, and double-click on the **Matinee** sequence to enter the Matinee editor. Right-click inside the **Group List** (the dark-gray column below all the tabs with text and to the left of the timeline. From the context menu that appears, click on **Add New Camera Group**. When prompted for a name, type in `Platform`.

> Alternatively, feel free to create an empty group and then add a new **Movement** track instead.

7. To create our moving platform, create two keyframes by clicking on the **Add Key** button at the beginning of the **Movement** track with the first at the **0:00** spot and the second one at the **1:00** spot. Then create another at the **6:00** spot. These keyframes won't be moving at all, so do not change their positions. Create two more keyframes at the **3:00** and **4:00** spots. At each of these keyframes move our platform along 640 pixels along the y axis. Once the first one is completed, you will have to adjust the second one to the same placement as well. Be sure to make the **Location** values match exactly.

> Specifying a time in which a keyframe should be reached is fairly simple. Click on the keyframe to select it, right-click, and then select **Set Time**; from there you can change any of the values you may need.

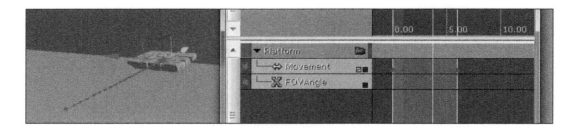

8. Now that we have a single platform already created, exit out of Matinee and exit this sequence. Copy and paste the sequence. Right-click on the newly created one and rename it to `Moving_Platform_UD`. Double-click on the new subsequence and enter its **Matinee** sequence. In this Matinee, change the **3:00** and **4:00** values to change on the z axis 256 units down.

    The point of going from a higher value to a lower value is to make the moving platforms meet up in such a way that you can jump on them for a period.

9. Make sure that the platform is selected in the editor. Exit out of the Matinee editor and click on the Matinee that you just finished editing. In the Matinee's properties, check the **Force Start Pos** option and set the **Force Start Position** value to `0.2`.

10. Select the three sides of the first platform that we created (the static one) and hold *Ctrl + G* in order to group them together. With our platforms created, let's remove some of the elements that are no longer needed and the default floor by selecting it with the left mouse button and hitting *Delete*. In its place, duplicate the group that we just made and position it on the same Z value as the floor that was there previously. In the same way as we created the group of the static platform, we can also use this same mesh to create a staircase. Have each stair only be 16 units above the previous one and create a staircase leading up to the initial static platform.

 Notice the capping mesh that I have placed covering the sides of the steps, otherwise they are likely to clip in and out of each other and look a bit gross.

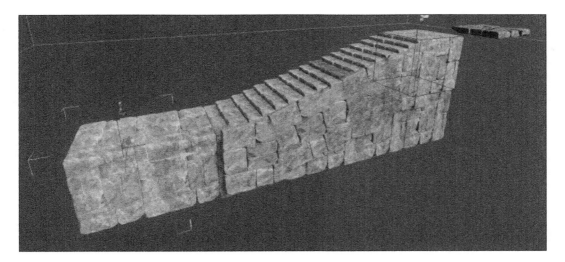

11. Click on our initial static platform and duplicate it to create floors for the moving platforms section, so that if the player falls they will not die so early in the level. Take the same group and duplicate it to the left of the player's starting position twice. Ungroup the groups we created by holding *Shift + G* and remove the inner parts that aren't required, then hold *Ctrl + G* to recreate the larger group as a whole. Delete the unused sections.

The stairs work, but the camera moves jaggedly as we walk up or down on it. Thankfully, we have an easy solution, the BlockingVolume brush.

For those needing a refresher, a **BlockingVolume** is simply an invisible brush that blocks players and other actors from traveling the stairs, and we can create a volume that will make the player actually move up a ramp when it looks like he is going upstairs.

It doesn't matter for this project, but a BlockingVolume allows zero extent traces (projectiles, rockets, and so on) to go through it.

Click on the builder brush (the red square in our initial level) and open up **Geometry Mode** by either selecting it on the right side on the top row of the **Modes** toolbar, or by pressing *Shift + 2*. With it selected, create a shape like the following screenshot, by first extending the left side of the brush outward, then grabbing the top-left points and dragging downwards until it is only 16 units above the original. Right-click on the brush and select **Add Volume | Blocking Volume**. At this point if you would like to select all of the stairs, change their **Collision Type** to **COLLIDE_NoCollision**, though it will not change what the player interacts with.

12. Duplicate our large left sidepiece twice on the right-hand side with the tallest section being the jump height from the up and down moving platform's peak. From there, create another duplicate object around 864 units apart and in the middle, place a duplicate of our initial static platform to use.

13. Click on the **LightmassImportanceVolume** option (the yellow box), and use **Geometry Mode** to extend it to the space that we are using in the level.

For those wondering, **Lightmass** creates light maps with complex light interactions, making the level look more lifelike. It is orthogonal to the rest of the rendering pipeline (dynamic lighting and shadowing), meaning it just replaces the light maps and static shadow maps with higher-quality ones.

The **LightmassImportanceVolume** option in a level controls the area that Lightmass emits photons in, allowing you to concentrate it only on the area that needs detailed indirect lighting. Areas outside the importance volume get only one bounce of indirect lighting at a lower quality.

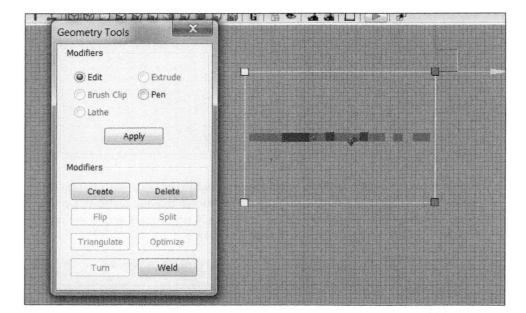

14. Build your project by selecting **Build | Build All**. Save your game using **File | Save All** and run our game by selecting **Play | In Editor**.

Objective Complete - Mini Debriefing

We have just replaced the default models in our level with different meshes to assemble parts that we can replicate. We also converted some of these meshes into Movers, and used Matinee in order to have our moving platforms actually move in the level using subsequences, which we can later turn into prefabs. We also created stairs that the player can climb while using BlockingVolumes in order to make the trip up less jarring.

Collecting collectables

As well as platforms, another staple of platformers is collectable items to reward players for exploring. We will implement two different types of collectable: items that the player may collect, and a power-up that will give the player the ability to double jump again.

Engage Thrusters

Now let's start adding in those collectables!

1. Go to the **Content Browser** window by going to **View | Browser Windows | Content Browser**. In **Content Browser**, find the following particle system: `ParticleSystem'WP_ShockRifle.Particles.P_WP_ShockRifle_Ball'` and click on it. Exit **Content Browser** and find a platform, right-click on it, and select **Add Emitter: P_WP_ShockRifle_Ball**. Hit the **Real Time** visualizer circled in the following screenshot or by pressing *Ctrl + R* to get a view of what our collectible will look like. Position the item in the air in a place that the player can reach by jumping, such as one of the previously mentioned positions the moving platform is travelling on.

2. Create a trigger around our new particle system by clicking on the builder brush. Right-click on the box selection on the **Brushes** toolbar and set the size of our builder brush to `64` in the **X**, **Y**, and **Z** positions. Drag the box to fit around the emitter that we created in the previous step, by using the translate tool or by holding *Ctrl* and dragging it to where we want it to be. Keep in mind to have it positioned along the axis so that the player will actually be able to touch it.

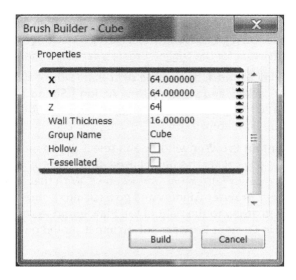

3. Back in the **Content Browser** window, find the particle system `ParticleSystem'WP_ShockRifle.Particles.P_WP_ShockRifle_Explo'` and add it slightly away from the first particle system. Inside its properties in **Particle System Component**, disable the **Auto Activate** option.

4. Open up the Kismet Editor and create a new subsequence by right-clicking and selecting **Create New Sequence : 0 Objs**. When the naming dialog comes up, type in `CoinPickup` for the **Sequence Name** field and press **OK**. Double-click on the sequence in order to enter it.

5. Outside Kismet, click on the trigger volume we created, then go back into Kismet. In our **CoinPickup** sequence, right-click and select **New Event Using TriggerVolume_0 | Touch** to create a **Touch** event for the **Trigger**. Create a variable under the **Instigator** output.

6. Next, create a **Play Sound** action on the right-hand side of the **Touch** event we just created by right-clicking and selecting **New Action | Sound | Play Sound**. Connect the **Target** input to **Instigator** from the **TriggerVolume_0 Touch** event that we created in the previous step.

7. Open up the **Content Browser** window and select the Sound Cue that you would like to play when you collect this item; I used `SoundCue'A_Pickups_Powerups.PowerUps.A_Powerup_UDamage_SpawnCue'`. With that Sound Cue selected, exit out of the **Content Browser** window and go back into Kismet to our subsequence. Click on the green arrow to the right of the **Play Sound** variable called the **Use selected object in Content Browser** button and it should be filled with the sound we want to use.

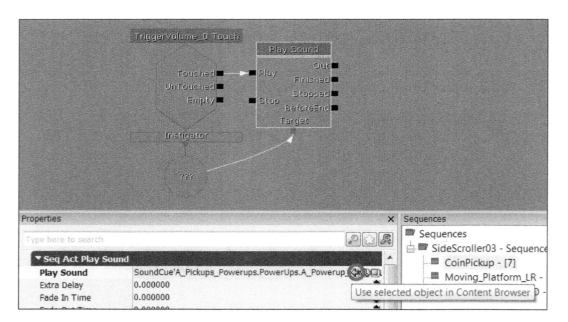

8. Create a new **Toggle Hidden** action by going into **New Action | Toggle | Toggle Hidden**. Connect the **Out** output from the **Play Sound** action to the **Hide** connection of the **Toggle Hidden** action.

9. Exit Kismet and in the UDK Editor click on the first particle system that we created (**Emitter_0**) and go back into Kismet. Right-click under the **Target** input and select **New Object Var using Emitter_0**.

10. Now create a new **Toggle** event by selecting **New Action | Toggle | Toggle**. Connect the **Out** from the **Toggle Hidden** action to the **Turn On** connection on the **Toggle** action.

11. Close Kismet and in the UDK Editor click on the other particle system that we created (**Emitter_1**) and go back into Kismet. Right-click under the **Target** input and select **New Object Var using Emitter_1**.

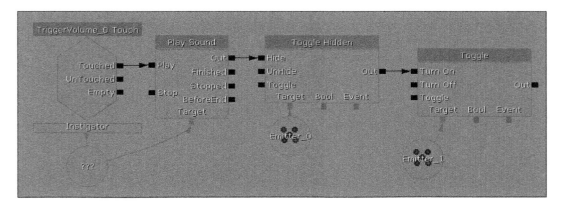

At this point, we should have a single collectable that will hide our coin and will then play a sound as well as a particle system to inform the player what has happened. Now that we have created a single coin, let's make it extremely easy for us to create new coins with the same functionality. To do that, we will be using prefabs.

12. Rotate your screen so that the sky is in the air and you can clearly see the objects of our collectable without touching anything else. Move your mouse to the top left, slightly away from where the top left of the collectible's objects are. Hold *Ctrl + Alt* and drag down, right until the red rectangle is completely covering our collectable. This should select everything within the collectable. Alternatively, you could hold down *Ctrl* and click on each of the elements to select them.

The marquee selection

A marquee selection is a quick way to select or deselect a group of actors within a certain area. This type of selection involves holding down a combination of keys, clicking one of the mouse buttons, and dragging the mouse cursor to create a box (colored red). All the actors within the box will be selected or deselected depending on the combination of keys and the mouse button that is clicked. The possible combinations and their effects are:

- *Ctrl + Alt* + click: Replaces the current selection with the actors contained in the box
- *Ctrl + Alt + Shift* + click: Adds the actors contained in the box to the current selection
- *Ctrl + Alt + Shift* + right-click: Removes any select actors in the box from the current selection

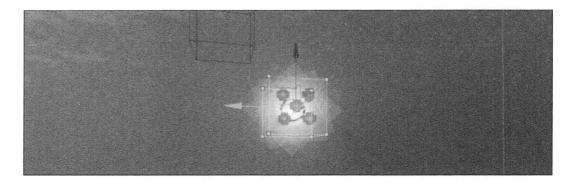

13. Right-click on the objects and select the **Create Prefab...** option. In the dialog box that comes up, put in Hotshot01 for the **Package** field and Coin for the **Name** section. After filling this out press the **OK** button. It will say that it found a sequence for the prefab. We say **Yes** to make the sequence part of the prefab and **No** to make the object an instance of the prefab. As soon as this happens, go to the **Content Browser** window and save our **Hotshot01** package in the same folder as your level.

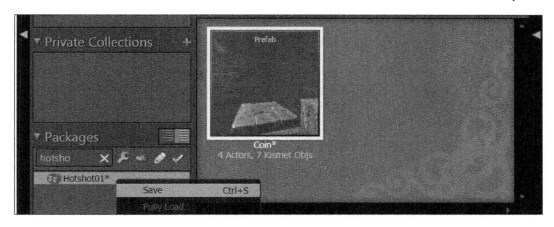

 Prefabs are very tricky and are prone to breaking while you're working on your projects. Be very careful when using prefabs, and save your file often after knowing that everything works.

14. Take time to place some of these prefabs into your levels in areas that players may want to visit or entice players to travel a certain way. Be sure to build your game before you see if they work by selecting **Build | Build All** from the menu.

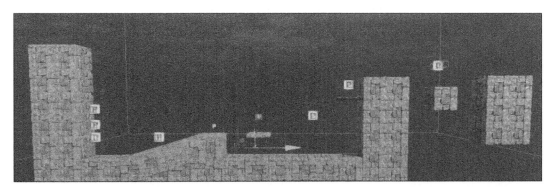

Note that some of these coins are obtainable with the player's default jump height. With that in mind, let's take our original actors to modify them for this new purpose.

15. Select the first emitter that we made on the collectable that is not currently a prefab. Press *F4* to access its properties and change the Particle System Component's **Template** property to be `ParticleSystem'CTF_Flag_IronGuard.Effects.P_CTF_Flag_IronGuard_Idle_Red'`. **Have the other emitter use** `ParticleSystem'VH_Scorpion.Effects.PS_Scorpion_Gun_Impact_Red'` **as its template.**

16. Right-click on one of the two emitters and select **Select Find Emitter_X** in Kismet. To the right of our **Toggle** action, we want to create a **Modify Property** action by right-clicking and choosing **New Action | Object Property | Modify Property** from the menus. Expand **Properties[0]**. In the **Property Name** variable type in `MaxMultiJump`. Check the **Modify Property** option and change the value of **Property Value** to 1. Connect the **Player** variable to the **Target** input. Connect the **Out** output from the **Toggle** action to the **In** input of the **Modify Property** action.

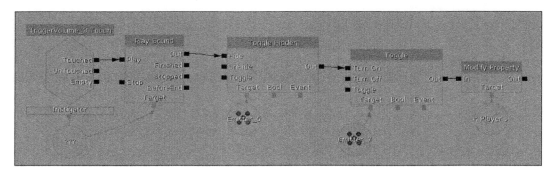

17. Back in the UDK Editor, select all of the objects that make our "Double Jump" power-up and press *Ctrl + G* to create a group of it. We only want to have one of these in our level and we want to make it somewhat skill-based in order to get it as it opens new areas for people to explore.

18. Build your project by selecting **Build | Build All**. Save your game using **File | Save All** and run our game by selecting **Play | In Editor**.

Objective Complete - Mini Debriefing

We have just created the first two objects of our platformer world. We created them using two particle systems connected together by a trigger volume, which executes some simple code. Once we created the base coin, we were then able to easily create duplicates with the same functionality by utilizing the power of the prefab. After this, we took our original and modified the particles it used, and then had it change the overall functionality of the game, enabling the player to jump further. Not too bad!

Classified Intel

Scott Rogers has a great primer on how to create effective platformer levels and how to place objects within the world called the Platformer Primer, which I recommend checking out if you want to start building levels of your own. The article is available at `http://mrbossdesign.blogspot.sg/2008/10/platformer-primer.html`.

Making the world come alive

Now that we have all of our mechanics in place, it would be a good time to spruce up our level a bit by adding some visual flair to it. In particular, we will be using the recent Landscape tool in order to build a backdrop for our level.

Engage Thrusters

Let's first add a landscape to create a backdrop for our level!

1. Click on the **Landscape** button under the **Modes** section of the left toolbar; this should cause the **Landscape Edit** window to open for us.

2. Once the **Landscape Edit** window comes up, it will have many options listed. We want to create a Heightmap, which we can now use within our level. In the **Heightmap Size** section, put in the values 64 x 64, and in the **Component Size** section select **put 7 quads per component**. Then click on the **Create Landscape** button.

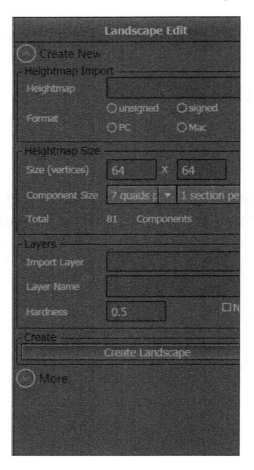

For more details about how landscapes are created and how sizes and dimensions are figured, UDN has some great information for you, which can be found at:

http://udn.epicgames.com/Three/LandscapeCreating.html

3. After waiting for a period, you should see a large checker board-looking plane, which is our landscape. All the tools in the **Landscape Edit** window have tool tips telling you what they are, but to get the general feel of it in order to raise the level of whatever you are currently selecting, you can hold *Ctrl* down and click. To lower the size of something, you can hold *Ctrl + Shift* and click. To change the brush's size, there is a variable under **Brushes** called **Brush Size**.

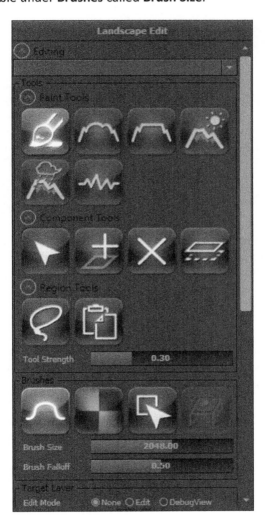

4. Create hills in the background of our level and lower the value of the areas that are actually part of the platforming section of our level. Be careful that the edges are not visible on the far left or far right of the level.

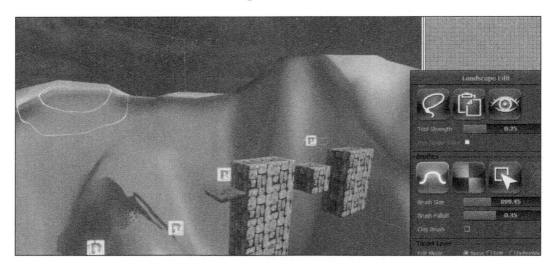

5. Exit the **Landscape** mode and enter **Camera Mode**, and then click on our landscape. Press *F4* to access the object's properties. Under **Landscape** in the **Landscape Material** variable, fill it with `Material'PivotPainterExamples.Materials. ground_Material'`; feel free, however, to fill it with whatever material would be best for your particular level.

It is possible for you to blend multiple materials together to create some really cool effects. If this interests you, check out the tutorial at the following link:

`http://www.polycount.com/forum/showthread.php?t=88347`

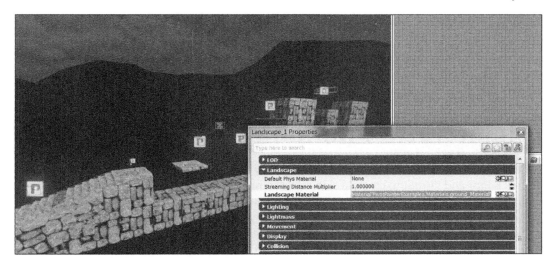

6. Build your project by selecting **Build | Build All**. Save your game using **File | Save All** and run our game by selecting **Play | In Editor**.

Objective Complete - Mini Debriefing

We have now taken our level and added a nice touch of background to make the world much more realistic as well as grounded. Due to the colors we used, it is very easy for us to see our player, the platforms, and the objects to grab; and though the background is distant, it seems real.

Mission Accomplished

In not much time, we have accomplished some very exciting things in UDK using just the Unreal Editor and Kismet to create a side-scrolling platform game. We created our own custom camera, which will follow our player when he is spawned, and modified the player with the use of the `.ini` files and Kismet to create some very interesting features. We then created our level's environment, by first creating a static platform and then moving on to dynamic ones. With those created, we made collectibles that the player can obtain, as well as one that actually gives the player additional functionality. Finally, we used **Landscape Mode** to create a backdrop for our game world. Let's take one final look at what we have accomplished:

You Ready to go Gung HO? A Hotshot Challenge

Our game is well on its way to being something special, but there are some things we could still add to make it even better! How about you take some time between projects and try to complete the following:

- ▶ Add background music to our world and more sound effects
- ▶ Add a door at the end of our level that will only open when we collect all of the coins in the level
- ▶ Whenever our player dies, reset the camera's position
- ▶ Create a basic enemy that will disappear if we jump on its head and move around in a fixed path
- ▶ Add health to our player; if he misses the head when hitting an enemy, damage him

Project 2
Terror in Deep Space

After that inviting trip back to yesteryear and the games that existed then, we now look to the stars. Ever since computers have entered our lives, we have used them to create simulations. Some of the very first real computer games made were based on *Star Trek*, where the player would be in charge of a spaceship controlling it and exploring the Universe. Other games such as *X-Wing* have taken this type of gameplay and given it more action, putting you into the cockpit of a ship, fighting as a part of an intergalactic war. Later, *Starfox* showed us how to do a barrel roll in a specific kind of game called a rail-shooter. Nowadays, we can see games where the players are controlling their own ship in MMOs, such as *The Old Republic* and *EVE Online*.

Now that we have a little background, a fitting second project would be to create our very own game set in the final frontier.

Mission Briefing

We will be creating a rail-shooter game, which is three-dimensional in nature, where the player controls a ship. This ship can move around the screen and shoot projectiles straight ahead. Enemies and obstacles will spawn towards the player and the player will avoid/shoot them.

This mission will be similar in terms of scope to the previous mission of getting functional gameplay using only the UDK Editor and Kismet.

Why Is It Awesome?

Once we finish this project, we will have experience in yet another game type that is not immediately associated with the Unreal engine. We will be able to create our very own rail-shooter game in the same vein as *Starfox*. We will also build on what we learned in the previous mission using similar functions to create a radically different kind of game.

Your Hotshot Objectives

This project will be split into five tasks. As we are not creating any advanced enemies in our game, we do not have to deal with UnrealScript in this project. It will be a simple and systematic process from the beginning to the end. Here is the outline of our tasks:

- ▶ Creating our level and camera
- ▶ Adding ship functionality (player movement)
- ▶ Adding particles to our level and ship
- ▶ Implementing obstacles
- ▶ Adding shooting and screen shaking

Mission Checklist

Before we start, let's make sure that we have replaced the `.ini` file, which we changed in the previous project, back to its previous state as this project may not work properly otherwise.

We will also need the art assets for our ship, skybox, and asteroids, including models and the textures to be applied to it. These can be downloaded from the support page from Packt Publishing's website at `www.packtpub.com/support`.

Creating our level and camera

A fitting start to our project would be to create a new level and populate the level with our camera in such a way as to create our rail-shooter game.

Prepare for Lift Off

Before we start working on the project, we must first create a new map. To do this, we must first select **File | New Level...** and from the pop up that comes up, select one of the top four options (I selected **Midday Lighting** this time, but it doesn't matter which one you choose as we will be replacing most of it).

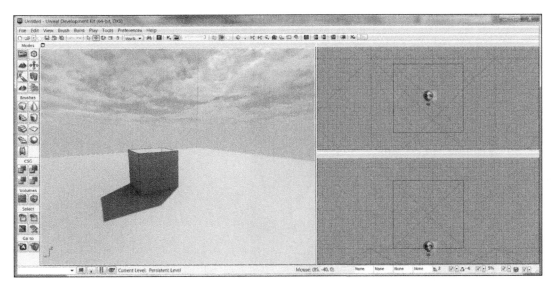

Engage Thrusters

Now that we have a base level to work on, let's start building our game!

1. Bring up the **World Properties** menu by selecting **View | World Properties** from the menu bar at the top of the UDK interface. Type `Game Type` in the search bar at the top of the **World Properties** menu, which will bring up the **Game Type** menu and the options relevant to us. From there, change the drop-down menus for both **Default Game Type** and **Game Type for PIE** to **UDKGame**. In the **Zone Info** section under **Kill Z**, set the value to `-1000`.

2. Right-click on the **Cube** icon on the left toolbar directly underneath the **Brushes** text. In the settings for the builder brush, check the **Hollow** option. This will create a hollow cube. Move the cube using the translate tool to the bottom-left of the screen from the Top viewport and raise it up in order to make it above the surface of the level. Click on the **Build** button and then add the geometry to our level by clicking on the **CSG_Add** option or by pressing *Ctrl + A*.

3. Put **PlayerStart** for the level inside the newly created box. If the object has a red X on it, move the object until it has plenty of space on all sides in order to spawn the player there. The X means that there is not enough space for the player to spawn in the area.

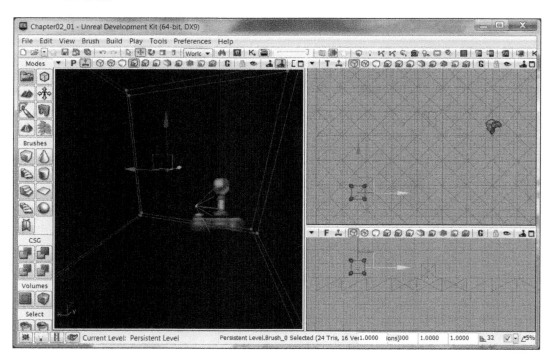

4. With the player taken care of, let's get our skybox working. Enter into the **Content Browser** window by either selecting its icon or by going to the **View** menu and selecting **Browser Windows | Content Browser**. Click on the **Import** button located in the bottom menu. Select all of the files within the `Chapter 2\Assets\Skybox` folder by clicking on one file, holding *Ctrl*, and selecting the other. With them selected, click on **Open**.

5. There will be an **Import** dialog that will come up. In the **Package** section, type in the name `Hotshot02` and confirm that `x_neg_skybox` is in the **Name** section and press **OK To All**. You should be brought back to the **Content Browser** window where you will see our new package with six new files.

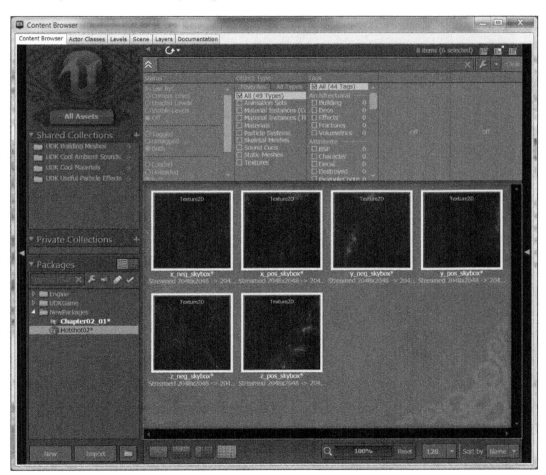

6. Right-click on the **Hotshot02** package and save it to the same location where you will save your map. With the package saved, right-click in the window and select **New TextureCube**. Inside the menu that pops up, confirm that the name Hotshot02 is in the **Package** section, and under the name of the file put in SpaceSkybox. There should be a new menu that pops up with many different selections. Inside the **Content Browser** window, click on the **x_pos_skybox** Texture2D and go back into the **SpaceSkybox** menu. Click on the green arrow pointing to the left of the **Face Pos X** option. Do this for the other five images matching the names between the two objects.

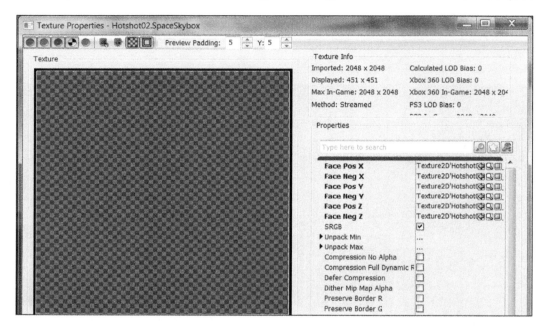

7. Exiting out of the TextureCube options, right-click in the same **Content Browser** window and select **New Material**. Inside the menu that pops up, confirm that the name `Hotshot02` is in the **Package** field, and under the name of the file put in `SpaceMaterial`. Right-click within the Material Editor and select **Parameters | New TextureSampleParameterCube**. Inside the **Content Browser** window, click on the **SpaceSkybox** TextureCube we created in the previous step and then select **Use selected object in Content Browser** on the **Texture** property of the newly created node.

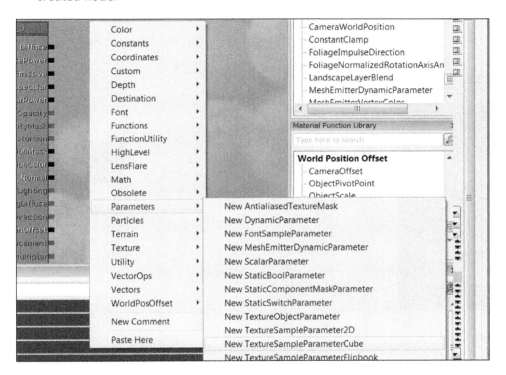

8. With the cube created, next we need to create a **Vector Transform** node by selecting **VectorOps | New Transform**. Connect **UVs** of **ParamCube** to the left-hand side of the **Vector Transform** node. To the right-hand side of **Vector Transform**, create a **Camera Vector** node by selecting **Vectors | New Camera Vector**. Connect **Camera Vector** to the right-hand side of **Vector Transform**. Finally, connect the black section of **ParamCube** to the connector on **Diffuse** of the material. You should see our texture on the left-hand side of the Material Editor. If you move it around, you will notice that it allows us to look at the six images we have imported like a panorama. Click on the green checkmark to save our changes and exit out of the Material Editor.

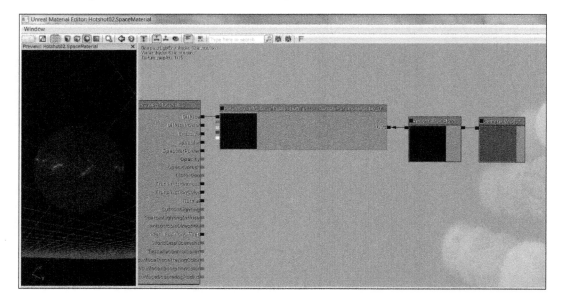

In the game industry, some engines create this effect by using something known as a **skybox**. The Unreal engine typically uses Skydomes to create these, but TextureCubes are not covered often enough and can be quite useful for things such as reflections.

9. Click on **SpaceMaterial** that we created in the **Content Browser** window. Inside our level, click on **ExponentialHeightFog** in the level and press the *Delete* key to delete it. You should notice that the sky becomes much clearer. Then, click on the Skydome located in our actual level. Press the *F4* key in order to access the object's Properties window. In the search bar above, start to type in the word `Material`. Inside the **Materials[0]** option, click on the green arrow to make the object replace its material with the one we created.

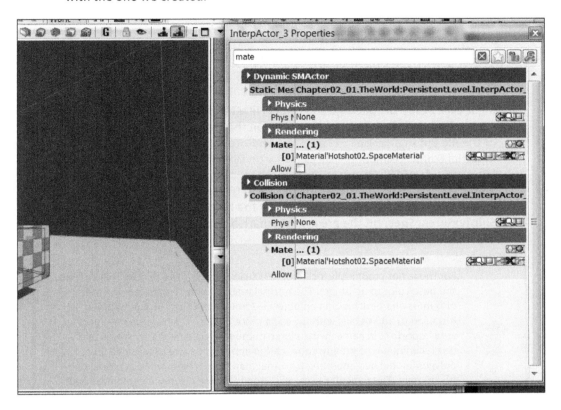

10. Save our **Hotshot02** package by right-clicking on it in the **Content Browser** window and selecting **Save**. Save your project (**File | Save All**).

11. Enter into the **Content Browser** window by either selecting its icon or going to the **View** menu and selecting **Browser Windows | Content Browser**. Click on the **Import** button on the bottom menu. Select all of the files within the `Chapter 2\Assets\Ship` folder by clicking on one file, holding *Ctrl*, and selecting the others. With them selected click on **Open**. There will be an **Import** dialog that will come up. In the **Package** field, confirm that the package is `Hotshot02` and that `Ship` is in the **Name** section and press **OK To All**. You should be brought back to the **Content Browser** window where you will see a static mesh as well as three texture files to use on it.

You may experience a `.fbx` warning due to the version exported; just click through it if it appears.

12. Right-click inside the package and select **New Material**. Inside the menu that pops up, confirm that the name `Hotshot02` is in the **Package** field, and under the name of the file put in `ShipMaterial`. Drag-and-drop the textures we imported into the Material Editor. Connect the black arrow on **Diffuse** with the black arrow on the left-hand side of **ShipTextures_Diffuse**. Then, connect the black arrow on **Normal** with the black arrow on the left-hand side of the **ShipTextures_Normal**. Finally, connect the black arrow on **Specular** with the black arrow on the left-hand side of **ShipTextures_Spec**. Hit the green checkmark on the top-left area in order to update the material.

For those not graphically inclined, a **Diffuse** texture is the texture that defines the base color of an object. The normal map is a way to *fake* the lighting of bumps and dents within an object—sometimes called **Bump mapping**. It is used to add details without using more polygons, which is something very important in games with a large number of objects. A common use of this technique is to greatly enhance the appearance and details of a low-polygon model by generating a normal map from a high-polygon model or height map. The **Specular** texture is used to define a surface's shininess and highlight color, with white being super shiny and black being zero shine. This is used in order to create detail to make our levels look more realistic.

The higher the value of a pixel (from black to white), the shinier the surface will appear in game.

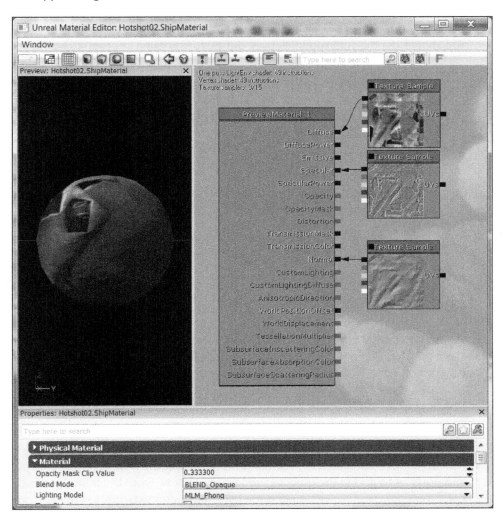

13. Save the package by right-clicking on the **Hotshot02** package and selecting **Save**. Then double-click on the static mesh for the ship. In the properties on the right-hand side, start typing in the word `Material`. In the **Content Browser** window, click on the ship material that we created and press the green arrow to load it into the ship. You should see the ship suddenly have our texture applied appropriately.

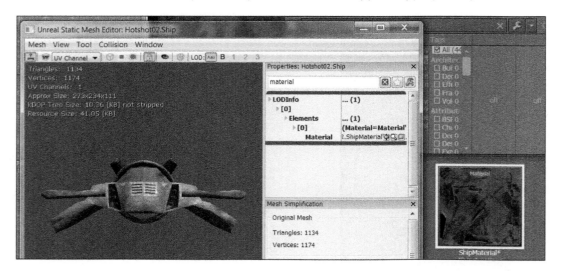

14. Still in the Static Mesh Editor, click on the **Collision | Auto Convex Collision** option. From there, click on the **Apply** button and wait for it to generate collision data for us. Erase the text in the property's search bar and make sure **Can Become Dynamic** is checked.

15. Close the Static Mesh Editor. In the **Content Browser** window, click on our ship's static mesh, close **Content Browser** and right-click inside our level on the ground, and select **Add InterpActor: Hotshot02.Ship** to put our ship into the level.

16. Now let's move our ship to its correct position. Select the newly created ship object and press *F4* to access the object's Properties window. From there, in the search bar, type `Location`. Once you find the **Location** vector variable, set the **X**, **Y**, and **Z** values to 0. Next, type `Rotation`. Make sure that the **Roll**, **Yaw**, and **Pitch** options are set to 0. You will notice that the ship looks like it disappeared; it has not, but it is inside the box provided by the default level. Delete the box mesh and the ground; we do not need it anymore.

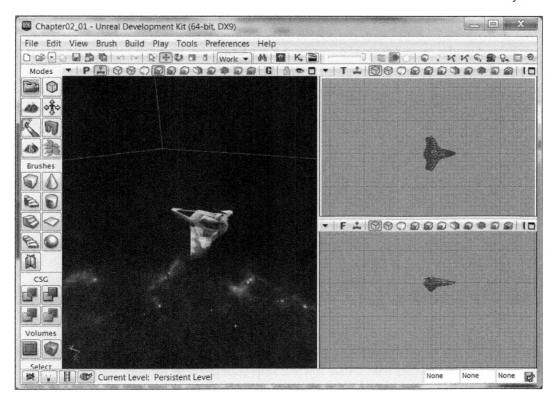

17. From this point, you are going to see some steps similar to that of the previous mission. We now need to access the **Actors Classes** panel by selecting **View | Browser Windows | Actor Classes**. Inside, click on the **CameraActor** selection.

18. Go back to the editor, right-click on the ship, and select **Add CameraActor Here**. With the object placed, press *F4* to go to the object's Properties menu. Change the value of **X** in the **Location** property to be 0, **Y** to be -500, and **Z** to be 250. Under **Rotation**, change **Yaw** to be 90 degrees and **Pitch** to be -11.25 degrees:

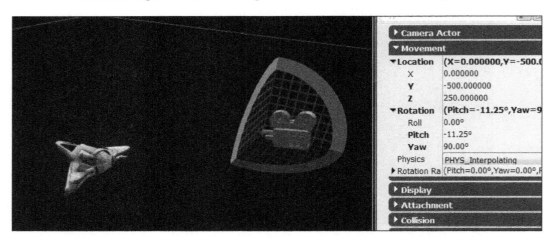

19. At this point, follow all of the same steps that we did in Kismet in the *Creating our level and camera* task from steps 5 to 9.

20. Save your project (**File | Save All**) and start your game by pressing *F8* or selecting **Play | In Editor** on the main toolbar.

Objective Complete - Mini Debriefing

We have just created a space level with a spaceship and camera using assets of our own creation. More specifically, we have imported custom content into the Unreal engine and are creating the interface for our new project.

Adding ship functionality

You may be wondering why I did not attach the camera to our spaceship object as in the previous project. For this project, I want to have a static camera with the ship moving within the bounds of our camera.

Engage Thrusters

With that in mind, let's start creating our player's movement.

1. Open up the Kismet Editor. Create a **Key/Button Pressed** event by right-clicking and selecting **New Event | Input | Key/Button Pressed**. Inside the node's properties under **Input Names** in the **[0]** place, put w and change **Re Trigger Delay** to 0.0.

2. Create a **Toggle** action by right-clicking and selecting **New Action | Toggle | Toggle**. Connect **Pressed** from the **Key/Button Pressed** event to the **Turn On** input of the **Toggle** action. Connect the **Released** output from the **Key/Button Pressed** event to the **Turn Off** input of **Toggle**. Under the **Bool** input, right-click and create a new **Bool** variable by selecting **Create New Bool Variable**. Inside the newly created bool's properties give it the name of MoveUp in the **Var Name** property.

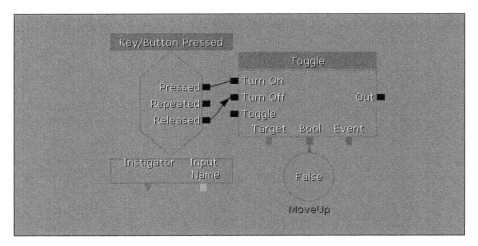

3. Copy and paste these nodes by selecting them all by holding down *Ctrl* and *Alt* and clicking slightly above and to the left-hand side of the **Key/Button Pressed** event and dragging till the red box that is created contains all of these elements. Once this is done hit *Ctrl + C* and then *Ctrl + V* to paste a copy of this into your level. Replace W in the **Input Names** place with S and change the word Up in the variable to Down. Do the same for **A** and **D** using Left and Right respectively.

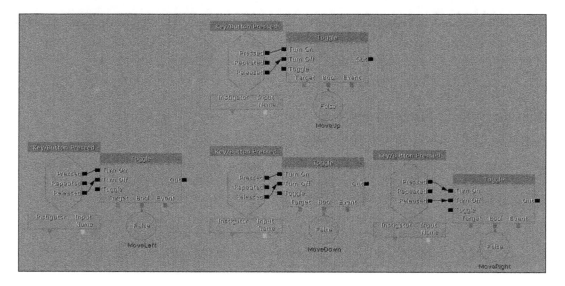

I personally laid the Kismet out as if it was using the WASD keys, but you could add in an event in the .ini files as we showed in the previous mission to make the code work with WASD, the arrow keys, or joysticks. For more information on how to do input similar to this with iOS devices, please check out my previous book with Packt Publishing, *UDK iOS Development Beginner's Guide*.

4. Next, right-click beside the **W** action and create a float variable by selecting **New Variable | Float | Float**. In the **Var Name** property give it a name of Speed and set its value to 5. This variable can be used to adjust the speed of our player to make them move quicker or slower depending on what we want.

5. Underneath our **Player Spawned** event create a remote event by right-clicking and selecting **New Event | Remote Event**. In the **Event Name** variable put in PlayerMovement.

6. Next to the **Set Camera Target** action that we created in the previous section, add an **Activate Remote Event** action by right-clicking and selecting **New Action | Event | Activate Remote Event**. Inside the **Event Name** variable put in PlayerMovement. You should see the red Xs change into green checkmarks once you press *Enter*. Connect the **Out** output of the **Set Camera Target** action to the **In** input of **Activate Remote Event 'PlayerMovement'**.

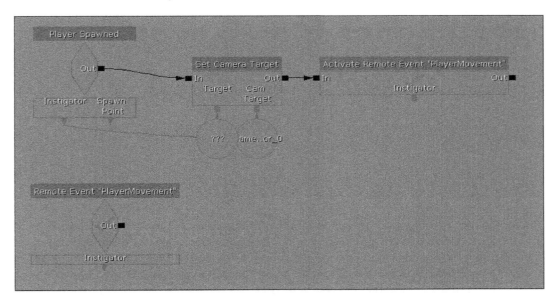

7. Create a **Get Location and Rotation** action by right-clicking and selecting **New Action | Actor | Get Location and Rotation**. Inside the editor, click on our ship **InterpActor**. Under the **Target** action of our **Get Location and Rotation** action, right-click and select **New Object Var Using InterpActor_0**. In the object's Properties window, give it a **Var Name** value of PlayerMesh. Underneath the **Location** variable right-click and select **Create New Vector Variable**. Connect the **Out** output from **Remote Event 'PlayerMovement'** to the **In** input of the **Get Location and Rotation** action.

8. Create a **Get Vector Components** action to the right-hand side of our **Get Location and Rotation** action by right-clicking and selecting **New Action | Math | Get Vector Components**. Connect the **Input Vector** to the **Location** vector we created in the previous step. Create two floats underneath the **X** and **Z** values and give them **Var Names** of `playerX` and `playerZ` respectively. Connect the **Out** output from the **Get Location and Rotation** action to the **In** input of the **Get Vector Components** action.

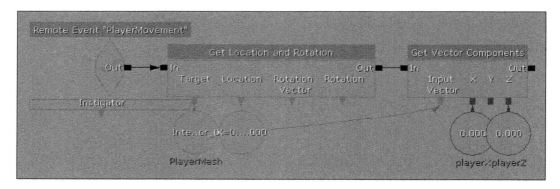

9. To the right-hand side of our **Get Vector Components** action, create a **Multiply Float** action by right-clicking and selecting **New Action | Math | Multiply Float**. In the **A** slot create a new float variable and set its value to `1.0`. On the **B** side, create **Named Variable** by right-clicking and selecting **New Variable | Named Variable** and putting in `Speed` in the **Name** section. You should see it change from a red X to a green checkmark. If not, make sure it matches the name of the float we created in step 4. In the **Float Result** section, create a new **Float** variable and give it a **Var Name** value of `Velocity`, which we will be using later.

10. To the right-hand side of the **Multiply Float** action, right-click and select **Create New Sequence : 0 Objs**. In the dialog that pops up, enter `GetDirectionInput` in the **Sequence Name** section and press **Enter**. This will create a subsequence that we will use in the next few steps. Double-click on the new sequence in order to enter it.

11. Create a **Sequence Activated** event by selecting **New Event | Sequence Activated**. To the right-hand side of it, create a **Compare Bool** comparison by right-clicking and selecting **New Condition | Comparison | Compare Bool**. Under the **Bool** variable, create **Named Variable** with the value of `MoveUp`, which we created in step 2.

12. Next to the **True** output of the **Compare Bool** comparison, create another **Compare Bool** conditional. In the **Bool** variable of this one, use a named variable with the value of `MoveLeft`. Connect the **True** output of the **MoveUp Compare Bool** comparison to the **In** input of **MoveLeft Compare Bool**.

13. Next to the **True** output of the **MoveLeft Compare Bool** comparison, create a **Finish Sequence** action by right-clicking and selecting **New Action | Misc | Finish Sequence**. In the **Output Label** variable, put in UpLeft. Connect the **True** output from **MoveLeft Compare Bool** to the **In** input of the **Finish Sequence "UpLeft"** action.

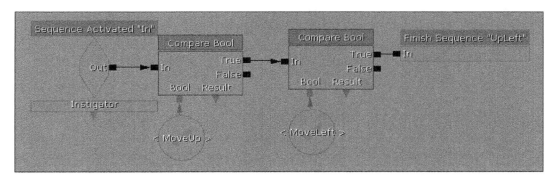

14. Now create a new **Compare Bool** comparison. In the **Bool** variable of this one, use a named variable with the value of MoveRight. Connect the **False** output of **MoveLeft Compare Bool** to the **In** input of **MoveRight Compare Bool**.

15. Next to the **True** output of the **MoveRight Compare Bool** comparison, create a **Finish Sequence** action by right-clicking and selecting **New Action | Misc | Finish Sequence**. In the **Output Label** variable, put in UpRight. Connect the **True** output from the **MoveRight Compare Bool** comparison to the **In** input of the **Finish Sequence "UpRight"** action.

16. Create another **Finish Sequence** action with the output level of Up and connect the **False** of **MoveRight Compare Bool** to the **In** input of the newly created **Finish Sequence "Up"**.

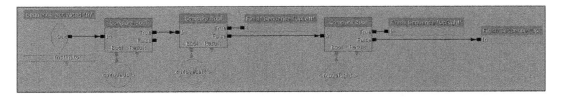

17. Now if we know that the player has not gone up in any way, we can check through the down key. To the right-hand side and below **MoveUp Compare Bool**, create a **Compare Bool** comparison by right-clicking and selecting **New Condition | Comparison | Compare Bool**. Under the **Bool** variable, create **Named Variable**, this time with the value of MoveDown.

18. Next to the **True** output of **Compare Bool (MoveDown)**, create another **Compare Bool** conditional. In the **Bool** variable of this one, use a named variable with the value of `MoveLeft`. Connect the **True** output of **MoveDown Compare Bool** to the **In** input of **MoveLeft Compare Bool**.

19. Next to the **True** output of the **MoveLeft Compare Bool** comparison, create a **Finish Sequence** action by right-clicking and selecting **New Action | Misc | Finish Sequence**. In the **Output Label** variable, put in `DownLeft`. Connect the **True** output from **MoveLeft Compare Bool** to the **In** input of **Finish Sequence "DownLeft"**.

20. Now create a new **Compare Bool** conditional. In the **Bool** variable of this one, use a named variable with the value of `MoveRight`. Connect the **False** output of **MoveLeft Compare Bool** to the **In** input of **MoveRight Compare Bool**.

21. Next to the **True** output of the **MoveRight Compare Bool** comparison, create a **Finish Sequence** action by right-clicking and selecting **New Action | Misc | Finish Sequence**. In the **Output Label** variable, put in `DownRight`. Connect the **True** output from **MoveRight Compare Bool** to the **In** input of **Finish Sequence "DownRight"**.

22. Create another **Finish Sequence** action with the **Output Label** variable of `Down` and connect the **False** output of **MoveRight Compare Bool** to the **In** input of the newly created **Finish Sequence "Down"** action. Now with Up, UpLeft, UpRight, Down, DownLeft, and DownRight completed, we only need to take care of Left and Right. Let's do that now.

23. Create a new **Compare Bool** comparison with `MoveLeft` in the **Bool** area. In the **True** section, connect **Finish Sequence** with `Left` as the **Output Label** variable. In the **False** section, connect another **Compare Bool** comparison with `MoveRight` in the **Bool** area. If **True**, connect **Finish Sequence** with `Right`. If **False**, create a **Finish Sequence** action with `None` as the value and connect it all together, as shown in the following screenshot:

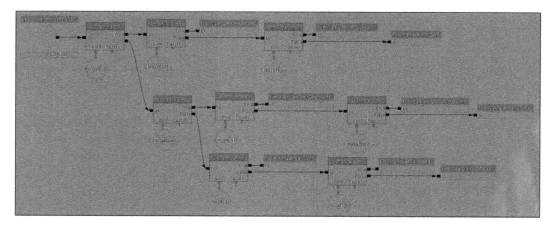

All of the Kismet that is created as well as all of the code given throughout this book are available on Packt Publishing's website for you to download, to make the project clearer.

24. Exit the subsequence. Inside the main sequence, connect the **Out** output from the **Multiply Float** action to the **In** input of our newly created **GetDirectionInput** subsequence.

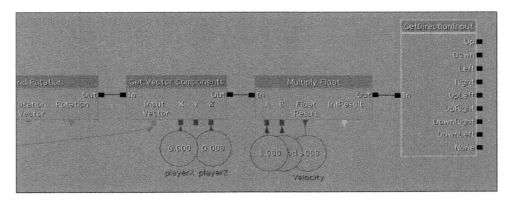

25. To the right-hand side of the **GetDirectionInput** subsequence, create two **Float** actions by right-clicking and selecting **New Action | Set Variable | Float**. In the **Target** sections, create two floats with **Var Names** of zMovement and xMovement respectively. In the **Value** section, create two floats with the value 1.0 for **zMovement** and 0.0 for the **xMovement** variable.

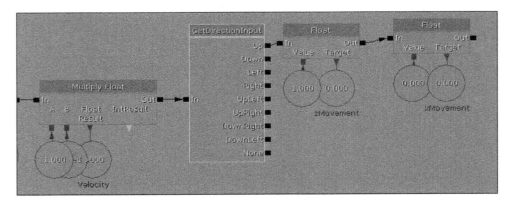

If you would like to adjust the order of the finish sequences in the **GetDirectionInput** subsequence just hold *Alt* down, and click and drag on the black box you would like to adjust. When you let go it will move it for you.

26. Copy (*Ctrl + C*) and paste (*Ctrl + V*) the two **Float** actions that we have created and change the **Target** sections to named variables with the **zMovement** and **xMovement** name. Change the value of **Float** that **zMovement** will be set to, from 1 to -1. Connect the **Down** output from the **GetDirectionInput** subsequence to the **In** input of the first of the two new floats being set.

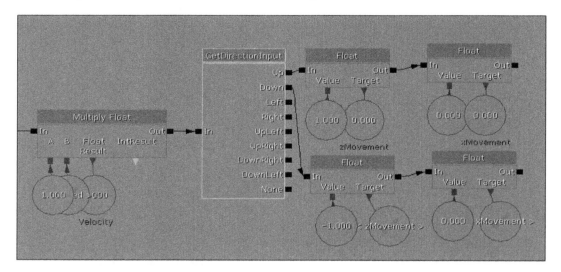

27. Use the following table to set the values for the other six choices:

Direction	zMovement	xMovement
Up	1	0
Down	-1	0
Left	0	1
Right	0	-1
UpLeft	0.707107	0.707107
UpRight	0.707107	-0.707107
DownRight	-0.707107	-0.707107
DownLeft	-0.707107	0.707107
None	–	–

In the end, you should wind up with something that looks like the following screenshot:

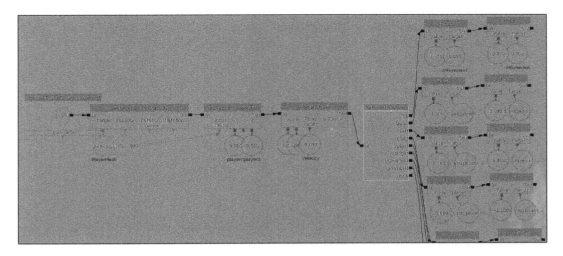

28. To the right-hand side of all of the floats being set, create a new subsequence with the name `MovePlayer`. Enter it by double-clicking on it.

29. Create a **Sequence Activated** event by selecting **New Event | Sequence Activated**. To the right-hand side of it create a **Multiply Float** action by right-clicking and selecting **New Action | Math | Multiply Float**. In the **A** slot create a named variable using **Velocity**. In the **B** slot create another named variable using **xMovement**. Create a new float inside the **Float Result** section. Connect the **Out** output from **Sequence Activated "In"** to the **In** input of the **Multiply Float** action.

30. To the right-hand side of the **Multiply Float** action, create an **Add Float** action by right-clicking and selecting **New Action | Math | Add Float**. In the **A** and **Float Result** slot, create two named variables using `playerX`. In the **B** slot, connect **Float Result** from the **Multiply Float** action. Connect the **Out** output from the **Multiply Float** action to the **In** input of the **Add Float** action.

31. Copy the **Multiply Float** and **Add Float** actions as well as the variables attached to them and paste them below the original actions, as in the following screenshot. In these newly created actions, change xMovement to zMovement and playerX to playerZ. Finally connect the **Out** output from **playerX Add Float** to the **In** input of **zMovement Multiply Float**.

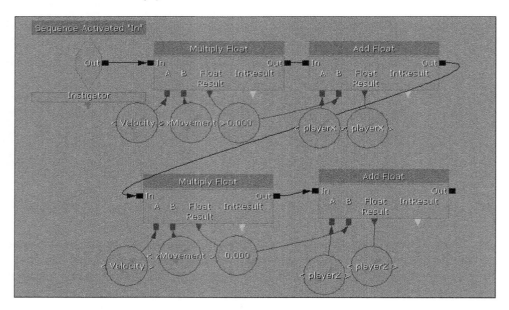

32. Create a **Set Vector Components** action below the **Multiply Float** and **Add Float** actions by right-clicking and selecting **New Action | Math | Set Vector Components**. Create a new vector for **Output Vector**. Create two named variables underneath the **X** and **Z** values and name them playerX and playerZ respectively. Connect the **Out** output from the **Add Float** action to the **In** input of the **Set Vector Components** action.

33. Create a **Set Actor Location** action by right-clicking and selecting **New Action | Actor | Set Actor Location**. Under **Target**, use the **PlayerMesh** named variable we created earlier in the project. Underneath the **Location** variable connect **Output Vector** from the previous node. Connect the **Out** output from the **Set Vector Components** action to the **In** input of the **Set Actor Location** action.

34. Finally, create a **Finish Sequence** action with the name of Out.

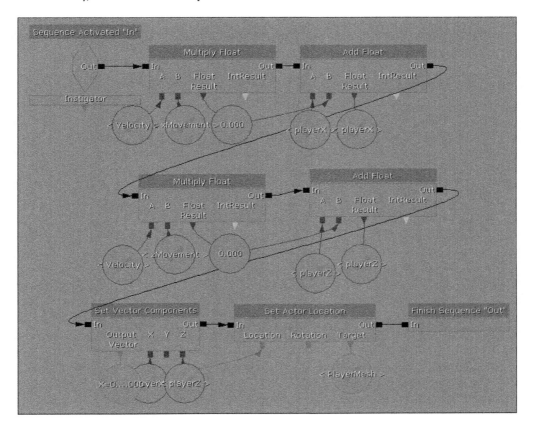

35. Exit this subsequence and enter the main sequence. To the right-hand side of our **MovePlayer** subsequence, add an **Activate Remote Event** action by right-clicking and selecting **New Action | Event | Activate Remote Event**. Inside the **Event Name** variable put in `PlayerMovement`. Right-click on the **In** black box on the **Activate Remote Event "PlayerMovement"** action and select **Set Activate Delay**. In the dialog that pops up, set the value to `.01` seconds and press **OK**. Connect the **Out** output from the **MovePlayer** subsequence and the **None** black box from the **GetDirectionInput** subsequence to the **In** input of **Activate Remote Event "PlayerMovement"**. Connect all the other **Out** outputs of the **Float** actions to the **In** input of the **MovePlayer** subsequence.

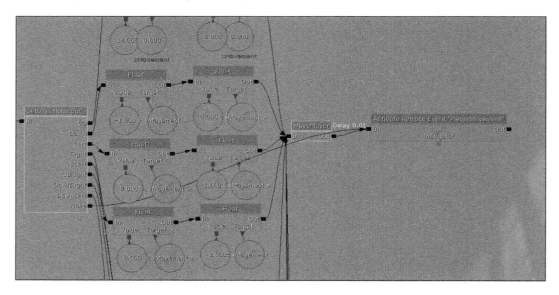

36. Save your project (**File | Save All**) and start your game by pressing *F8* or selecting **Play | In Editor** on the main toolbar.

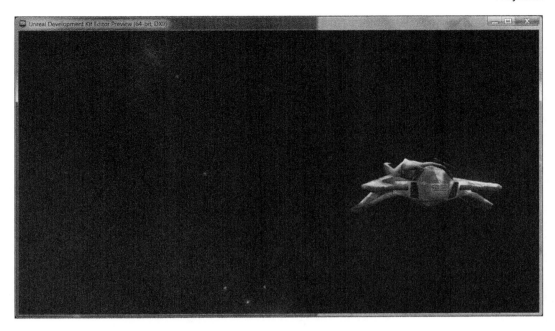

Objective Complete - Mini Debriefing

Whew! That was quite a lot of effort, but it definitely paid off. Right now we have accomplished what is probably going to be the most difficult part of our project, enabling the player to interact with the world to make our rail-shooter game much more exciting, and behind the scenes we've made our project with the correct calculations in mind for the future.

Classified Intel

At first glance it may appear as if I'm doing a lot of extra work in order to get the output that we've achieved, and you may be wondering why exactly I'm using 0.707107 so often when moving in diagonals. This is simply because no matter what the player puts into their controller, we want to be able to move the same distance. Moving 1 unit in both the up direction and the right direction will actually move us 1.414 (square root of 2) units, which we can figure out using the Pythagorean theorem. Doing the math, moving 0.707107 units in both the horizontal and vertical space moves us the same amount as if we were only moving one way. When we get into programming using UnrealScript, you will see how simple it would be to do actions very similar to what we did here in much less time, but it is nice to know that Kismet allows us the ability to prototype functionality like this.

Ship particles

Now that we have our ship functioning at least somewhat properly, let's add some polish to it and give our players the sense that they are moving through space.

Engage Thrusters

To do this, we are going to make use of one of Unreal's best features, its particle systems.

1. Open the **Content Browser** window by going to **View | Browser Windows | Content Browser**. Go to the **Hotshot02** package that we created at the beginning of this mission. Inside its window right-click and select **New ParticleSystem**. In the dialog that comes up give it the name `ShipSpeed`.

2. In the **Required** section of **Particle Emitter**, set the **Material** value in the Properties window to `Material'WP_Enforcers.Materials.M_WP_Enforcers_Impact_light'`. Next set the **Screen Alignment** value to **PSA_Velocity**.

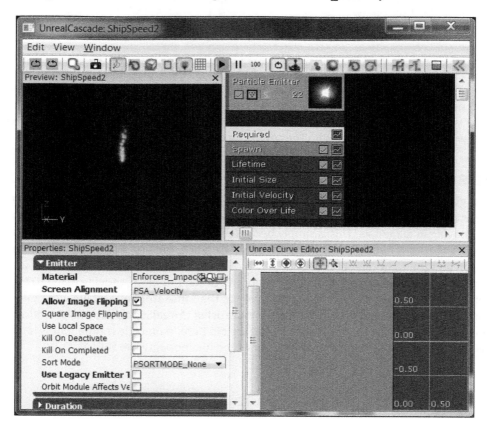

3. In the **Initial Velocity** section inside the **Min** section, use the **X**, **Y**, and **Z** values of 0, -2048, and 0. In the **Max** section, use 0, -4096, 0.

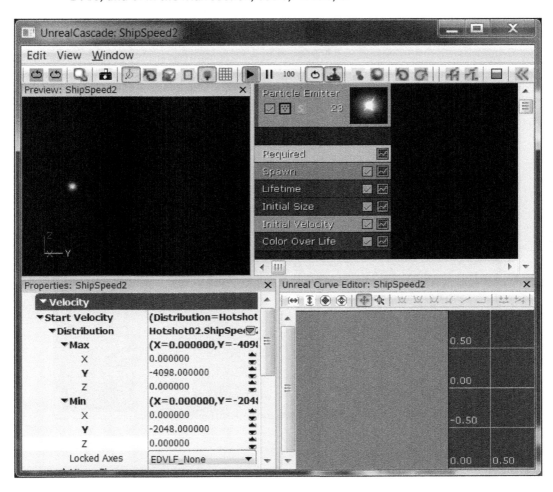

4. Underneath the **Color Over Life** section, create a **Size By Velocity** element by right-clicking and selecting **Size | Size By Velocity**. Inside the **Constant Distribution** value, change the values of **X**, **Y**, and **Z** to .02, .4, and .02.

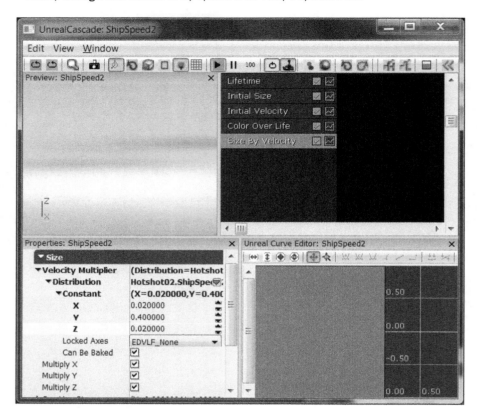

5. Next, go to the **Initial Size** section and change all the **Max** and **Min** values to 0.2 in the **X**, **Y**, and **Z** values.

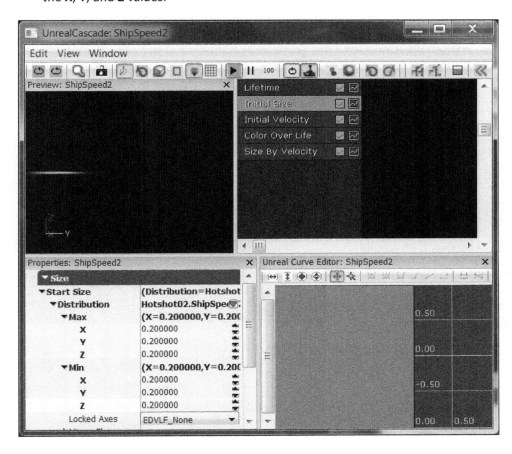

6. Underneath the **Size By Velocity** section, create a **Initial Location** element by right-clicking and selecting **Location** | **Initial Location**. Inside the **Max** section change the **X**, **Y**, and **Z** values to 512, 2000, and 512. In the **Min** section change the values of **X**, **Y**, and **Z** to -512, 2000, and -512. Then rotate the preview so that you can see it with the y axis facing away from us, and you'll see what the particle system will look like in our project.

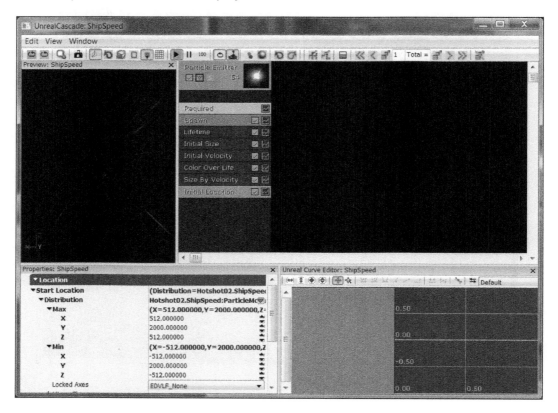

7. Exit out of the particle editor, select **ParticleSystem** in the **Content Browser** window, and exit back to the menu. Right-click on our ship and select **Add Emitter : ShipSpeed**; you should notice that when we play the game it will now look like the ship is traveling, when in reality it is not. What would really sell the illusion, however, would be to have some thrusters coming out of the ship. With that in mind, let's do just that!

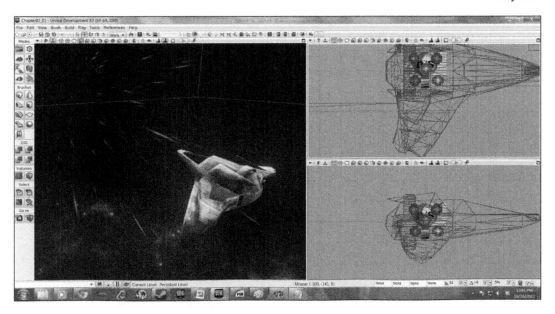

8. Return to the **Content Browser** window and find the particle system `ParticleSystem'VH_Manta.Effects.PS_Manta_Projectile'`. With that selected, go back into the game, right-click on the ship, and select **Add Emitter : PS_Manta_Projectile**. Press *F4* to enter the emitter's properties. Change the **Scale** value in the **Primitive Component** section to 0.5. Rotate the emitter by 90 degrees so that it is facing the same way as a thruster would on the ship, and use the translate tool to place the jet inside one of the six vents that are on the ship. (Use [to decrease the grid size or disable it all together). Click on the lock icon in the top-left corner of the Properties window and then type in the word base in the search bar. Click on the ship and then click on the green arrow to attach the particle system to that object.

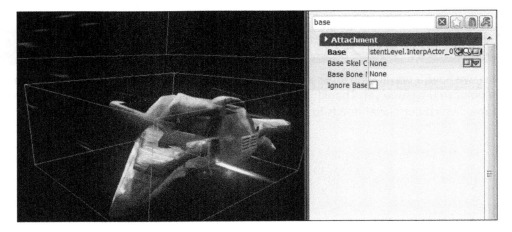

9. Press *Alt* and drag to create five other particles and position them according to how they would be positioned in the model.

10. Build your project by selecting **Build | Build All**. Save your game using **File | Save All** and run the game by selecting **Play | In Editor**.

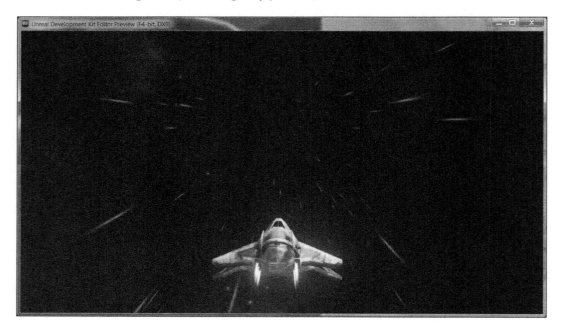

Objective Complete - Mini Debriefing

With a few little tweaks, we have now created a much more polished and professional-looking project. We now have the thrusters working on the back of our ship, and we also have moving stars via another particle system that we created from scratch using just a material.

Avoiding obstacles

So now, we have a player who looks pretty awesome and can move around, but there is not much point to the game yet. Thankfully, we will fix that in a moment as we add asteroids to our game, which our player needs to avoid.

Engage Thrusters

Now, let's add in some obstacles!

1. Import all four files from the `Asteroid` folder in the assets we provided. Right-click in the same **Content Browser** window and select **New Material**. Inside the menu that pops up, confirm that the name `Hotshot02` is in the **Package** section and under the **Name** section put in `AsteroidMaterial`.

2. Drag-and-drop the **android_diffuse**, **asteroid_normal**, and **asteroid_specular** textures and connect them to the appropriate slot as shown in the following screenshot. Click on the green checkmark and exit out of the Material Editor.

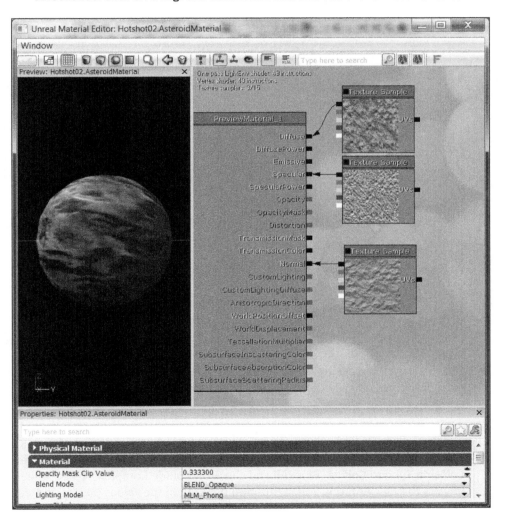

3. Back in the **Content Browser** window, double-click on the asteroid mesh. Check off **Can Become Dynamic** and type in `material` in the properties bar. Select **AsteroidMaterial** in the **Content Browser** window by clicking on it and click on the green arrow in order to set it as the material for the object. Create a collision for the object by clicking on the **Collision | Auto Convex Collision** option. From there click on the **Apply** button and wait for it to generate collision data for us.

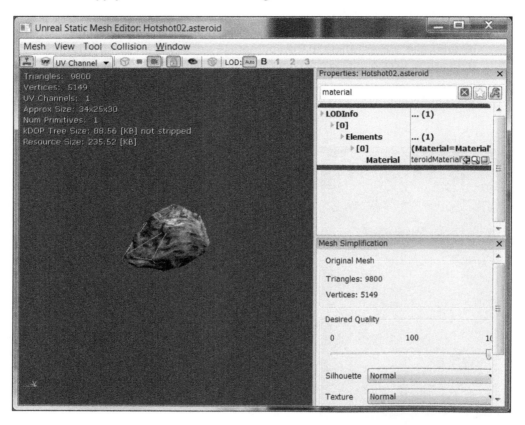

4. Exit the Static Mesh Editor. Back into the main editor, click on our ship once again. In its properties, change **Collision Type** to **Collide_BlockAll** and check **Collide Complex** on.

5. Add in the newly created asteroid to our level by dragging-and-dropping it into the world. Position the asteroid far away from the player, but once we create our Kismet subsequence, it will take care of the positioning for us. In its properties change **Collision Type** to **Collide_BlockAll** and check off **Collide Complex**. Next change the **Physics** to **Phys_Rotating** and in **Rotation Rate** put in the values `20`, `20`, and `20`.

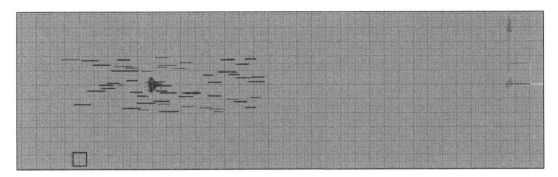

6. Go to the **Content Browser** window and find the particle system `ParticleSystem'Envy_Effects.VH_Deaths.P_VH_Death_SpecialCase_1_Base_Far'` and select it to use when the asteroid is destroyed, and put it slightly in front of our asteroid in the eyes of the player. Then make the emitter's base be the asteroid.

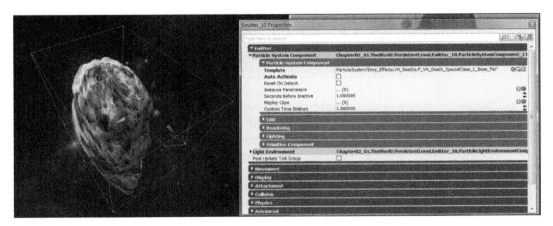

7. With your new asteroid selected by clicking on it, open up Kismet and create a new subsequence named `Asteroid`. Inside it first create a Touch event using the **Asteroid** subsequence by right-clicking and selecting **New Event Using InterpActor_1 | Touch**. In the **Class Proximity Types** section, make the **[0]** variable to be equal to `Actor`. Change the **Max Trigger Count** value to `0`, the **Re Trigger Delay** value to `0.0`, and uncheck **Player Only**.

8. Underneath the Touch event create a **Take Damage** event by right-clicking **New Event Using InterpActor_1 | Damage**. Change the **Damage Threshold** value to `0.1`, the **Max Trigger Count** value to `0`, and uncheck **Player Only**.

9. Inside the editor, click on the emitter we created in step 6. Create a **Toggle** event by right-clicking and selecting **New Action | Toggle | Toggle**. Underneath **Target**, connect our emitter, then connect the **Touched** and **Out** black boxes from the **InterpActor_1 Touch** and **InterpActor_1 Take Damage** events to the **Turn On** input of the **Toggle** action.

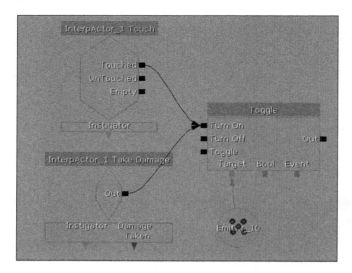

10. Above these two events, create a **Level Loaded** event by right-clicking and selecting **New Event | Level Loaded**. To the right-hand side of it create a **Set Vector Components** action by right-clicking and selecting **New Action | Math | Set Vector Components**. Create a new vector for the **Input Vector** section. Create a regular float variable on the **Y** spot with a value of 16300.0. On the **X** and **Z** options, create two random floats by selecting **New Variable | Float | Random Float** with a **Min** value of -300 and a **Max** value of 300 for the value under **X**, and a **Min** value of 100 and a **Max** value of 300 for the value under **Z**. Now connect the **Loaded and Visible** black box from the **Level Loaded** event to the **In** input of the **Set Vector Components** action.

11. To the right-hand side of the **Set Vector Components** action create a **Set Actor Location** action by right-clicking and selecting **New Action | Actor | Set Actor Location**. Connect **Output Vector** from the previous action to **Location** of this node. Under the **Target** variable select the asteroid in the editor and then create a variable using it. Connect the **Out** output from the **Set Vector Components** action to the **In** input of the **Set Actor Location** action.

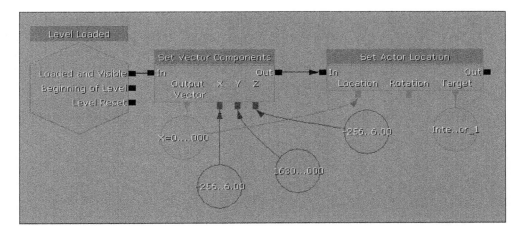

12. To the right-hand side of that, create a **Get Location and Rotation** action. Use the asteroid as its **Target** and a new vector variable for **Location**. To the right-hand side of it, create a **Get Vector Components** action and create three new float variables underneath the **X**, **Y**, and **Z** sections and connect **Location** from the previous action to **Input Vector** for this node. Connect the **Out** output from the previous node to the **In** input of the current node.

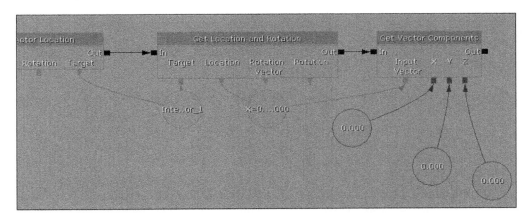

13. After that, to the right-hand side of the **Get Vector Components** action create a **Multiply Float** action. In the **A** section create a float with a value of -10. In **B** create a named variable with the name of Speed. In the **Float Result** output create a new float. Connect the **Out** output from the previous node to the **In** input of the current node. Next to that, create an **Add Float** action with the **Y** value from the **Get Vector Components** action as the **A** and **Float Result** variables. Inside **B** put **Float Result** from the **Multiply Float** action. Connect the **Out** output from the previous node to the **In** input of the current node.

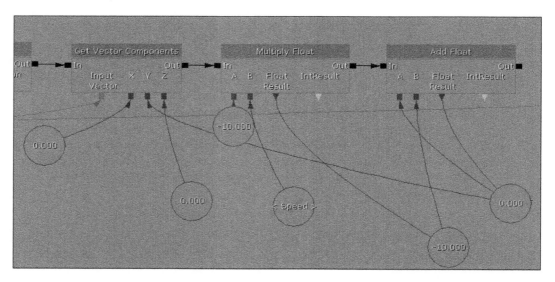

14. To the right-hand side of the **Add Float** action, create a **Set Vector Components** action and put the previously acquired **X** and **Z** values from the **Get Vector Components** action we've already gotten earlier in this section. In the **Y** section use **Float Result** from the previous **Add Float** action and create a new vector for **Output Vector**. Connect the **Out** output from the previous node to the **In** input of the current node. To the right-hand side of that, create a **Set Actor Location** action with **Object** being our asteroid mesh and the location being **Output Vector** from the **Set Vector Components** action we created. In the properties, uncheck the **Set Rotation** option. Connect the **Out** output from the previous node to the **In** input of the current node. Finally create a **Compare Float** comparison with **A** being the current **Y** value and **B** being -200. Connect the **A <= B** option to the first **Set Vector Components** action using the random numbers to reset our asteroid's position as it has passed the player. In the **A > B** option, connect it to the **Get Location and Rotation** option that will continuously move the asteroid towards the player.

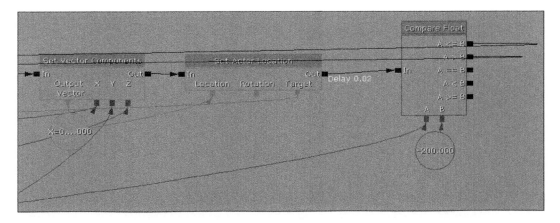

As an overview of what the entire `asteroid` subsequence should look like, please refer to the following screenshots:

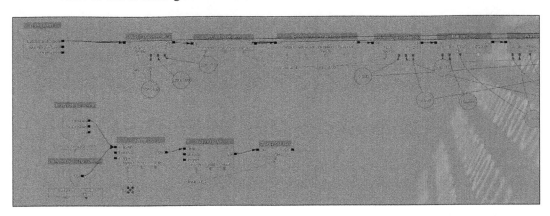

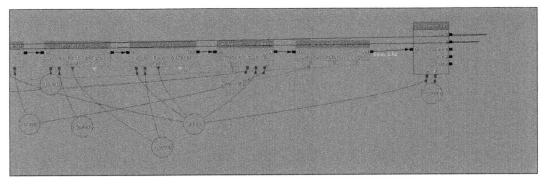

15. Build your project by selecting **Build | Build All**. Save your game using **File | Save All** and run our game by selecting **Play | In Editor**.

Objective Complete - Mini Debriefing

Not too shabby—we now have asteroids coming at us. More specifically, we have imported our own custom assets and assigned custom behavior to it making use of more particles. Now it would be fairly easy to turn this single asteroid into a prefab and just use a slight delay between each of the asteroids being run at the beginning of the **Level Spawned** event and slightly increase the speed to be more challenging over time. However, that is best left as a task for you to make your game project the way you wish to make it.

Shooting and screen shaking

We have many mechanics in place, but there is still one last thing missing in our rail-shooter game – the shooter part. Therefore, in this section we add some additional functionality to our player to provide the ability to shoot and feel impacts with asteroids.

Engage Thrusters

In order to shoot the asteroids, we first need to have something to fire at. In this case, we will be using projectiles. Let's set that up now.

1. Go to the **Actor Classes** window and find the **PathNode_Dynamic** class, and create two of those objects in front of one side of the ship from where you would like the ship to fire its weapons. Make sure that they are facing towards the direction where they should go. In the properties for both the objects, make their **Base** the ship's mesh and check **Destination Only** in the **Navigation Point** section.

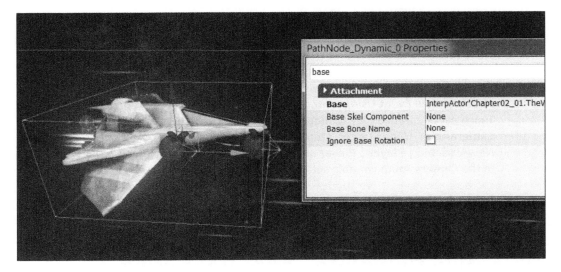

2. Go to Kismet and create a **Key/Button Pressed** action as we did when we were creating the player's controls. Under **Input Names [0]** put in SpaceBar; I also changed the **Re Trigger Time** value to 0.4. To the right-hand side of the **Key/Button Pressed** action create two **Get Location and Rotation** actions. Use first **Target** as the PathNode that is closest to the ship, and the second with the second. Connect **Pressed/Repeated** to the **In** input of the first **Get Location and Rotation** action. Connect the **Out** output for the first node to the **In** input of the second. To the right-hand side of the second **Get Location and Rotation** action, create a **Spawn Projectile** action by right-clicking and selecting **New Action | Spawn Projectile**. Under the **Projectile** class, use UTProj_Rocket.

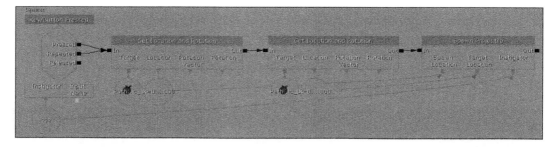

3. Outside Kismet, click on your ship and go back into Kismet. Underneath the logic that we just created, create a Touch event for our object by right-clicking and selecting **New Event Using : InterpActor_0 | Touch**. To the right-hand side of the Touch event create a **Play CameraAnim** action by selecting **New Action | Play CameraAnim**. Under **Target**, create a **Player** variable by right-clicking and selecting **New Variable | Player | Player** and in the Properties window unchecking **All Players**. In the **Camera Anim** variable set the value to CameraAnim'Envy_Effects. Camera_Shakes.C_VH_Death_Shake'.

4. Build your project by selecting **Build | Build All**. Save your game using **File | Save All** and run the game by selecting **Play | In Editor**.

Objective Complete - Mini Debriefing

Our player now has the ability to shoot and we now have an effect if the player ever gets hit by an asteroid. And with that, we now have all of the fundamentals in place for you to extend this project into any kind of rail-shooter experience that you'd be interested in, with a lot of effects and interactions.

Mission Accomplished

In not much time, we have completed some very exciting things in UDK using just the Unreal Editor and Kismet to create all the features needed for a rail-shooter game. We used TextureCubes and the Material Editor to create a custom space backdrop for our game and a static camera with a custom spaceship. We gave the spaceship the ability to move around using the arrow keys, giving the player movement in eight directions moving at the same rate at all angles. With that created, we added asteroids that fly towards the player, which they have to avoid and shoot. Finally, we actually implemented the ability to shoot using PathNodes and Kismet in order to create projectiles and shake the screen upon collision with asteroids. Let's take one final look at what we have accomplished:

You Ready to go Gung HO? A Hotshot Challenge

Our game is well on its way to being something special, but there are some things we could still add to make it even better! How about you take some time between projects and try to complete the following:

- ► Add background music to our world and more sound effects
- ► Add a second set of guns to our ship
- ► Increase the speed subtly while the game is being played in order to ramp up the difficulty over time
- ► Use fracture meshes to actually destroy the asteroids we create
- ► Use the collectables in the previous sections to give the player a temporary speed boost

Project 3

Terror in Deep Space 2: Even Deeper

Here we are at the next part of our exciting rail-shooter game project. In the previous project, we started making what could be a fantastic rail-shooter to play, but there were still a number of things that were missing for it to be considered an actual game. In this project, we are going to continue with our rail-shooter game by adding in functionality to make this much closer to a fully fledged game with new aspects such as health, enemies, and dying conditions!

With that in mind, let's get started.

Mission Briefing

Continuing along the same path as the previous project, we will use the basis of the project created in *Project 2*, *Terror in Deep Space*, to expand upon by adding enemies that shoot as well as a multitude of asteroids for the player to avoid and/or shoot.

We will also add additional functionality that can be added to practically any game for adding polish such as an HUD, opening cutscene, and Game Over state.

Why Is It Awesome?

Once we finish this project, our game will have multiple asteroids to fill out the game world as well as an opening cutscene, which will add a much more cinematic and polished feel to the game. The player will also have enemies to fight against and an in-game HUD system that tracks our player's health as well as the implementation of a Game Over state, which brings us just a few steps away from having the project be a fully fleshed-out game.

Your Hotshot Objectives

This project will be split into four tasks. Since we are not creating any advanced enemies in our game, we don't have to deal with UnrealScript in this project. It will be a simple step-by-step process from the beginning to the end. The following is an outline of our tasks:

- ▸ Creating multiple asteroids
- ▸ Spawning enemies
- ▸ Opening cutscene
- ▸ Player's health/HUD system

Mission Checklist

Before we start, let's make sure that we have completed the tutorial in the previous project because this one assumes that you did. If not, go to *Project 2, Terror in Deep Space*, and start from there.

We will also need the art assets for our enemy ship, including the models and the textures to be applied to it. These can be found on Packt Publishing's website at:

`http://www.packtpub.com/support`

Creating multiple asteroids

Since we created a set of asteroids, let's now enhance them and make it so that we can have many different asteroids coming at our players, but before we do that, let's update the logic and turn them into prefabs.

Prepare for Lift Off

Before we start working on the project, we must have completed the previous project's mission as it will be the base for this project. If you have not created it previously, please obtain the files from the `Chapter 2` folder located at Packt Publishing's website, go to **File | Open**, and select the file.

Engage Thrusters

Now that we have a base level to work from, let's start building our game!

1. Using the file from the previous project, open up Kismet and go to the **Asteroid** subsequence. From there go to the **InterpActor_1 Touch** and **InterpActor_1 Take Damage** events. To the right-hand side of the **Toggle** action, create a **Toggle Hidden** action by right-clicking and selecting **New Action | Toggle | Toggle Hidden**. Connect **Target** of the **Toggle Hidden** action to the emitter we used in the **Toggle** action and connect the **Out** output from the **Toggle** action to the **Unhide** input of the **Toggle Hidden** action.

2. Create a second **Toggle Hidden** action next to the right-hand side of the first **Toggle Hidden** action. Select our asteroid within our level, right-click under **Target** back in Kismet, and select **Create New Object Var with InterpActor_1**. Then connect the **Out** output from the first **Toggle Hidden** action to the **Hide** input of the second **Toggle Hidden** action. Right-click on the **Hide** input and give it a delay of 0.2 seconds by selecting **Set Activate Delay**.

3. To the right-hand side of the second **Toggle Hidden** action, create a **Change Collision** action by right-clicking and selecting **New Action | Actor | Change Collision**. In the Properties window, change the **Collision Type** variable to **COLLIDE_NoCollision** and connect the **Out** output of the **Toggle Hidden** action to the **In** input of the **Change Collision** action. Connect **Target** of the **Change Collision** action to **InterpActor_1**.

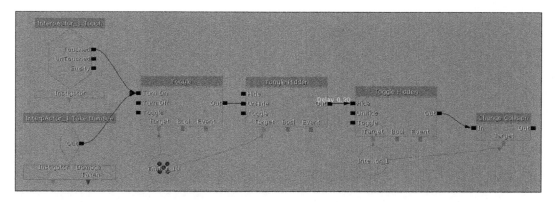

4. Above the **Level Loaded** event, create a **Set Vector Components** action by right-clicking and selecting **New Action | Math | Set Vector Components**. Create a new vector for **Output Vector**. Create three new random float variables by right-clicking and selecting **New Variable | Float | Random Float**. Inside their Properties window, set the **Min** value to 0 and the **Max** value to 360.

5. To the right-hand side of the newly created **Set Vector Components** action, create a **Toggle Hidden** action by right-clicking and selecting **New Action | Toggle | Toggle Hidden**. Click on the explosion emitter on the asteroid and come back to Kismet and set it as **Target**. Connect the **Out** output from the **Set Vector Components** action to the **Hide** input of the **Toggle Hidden** action.

6. To the right-hand side of that, create a **Toggle** action by right-clicking and selecting **New Action | Toggle | Toggle**. Under **Target**, use the asteroid **InterpActor_1**. Connect the **Out** output from the **Toggle Hidden** action to the **UnHide** input of the **Toggle Hidden** action.

7. Next, create a **Change Collision** action by right-clicking and selecting **New Action | Actor | Change Collision**. In the Properties window change the **Collision Type** variable to **COLLIDE_BlockAll** and connect the **Out** output of the **Toggle Hidden** action to the **In** input of the **Change Collision** action.

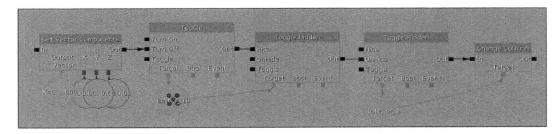

8. To the right-hand side of the **Change Collision** action, create a **Float** action by right-clicking and selecting **New Action | Set Variable | Float**. For **Target**, select the **-10** value in the **Multiply Float** action that we created previously. Under **Value**, create a random **Float** variable with values ranging from -10 to -25.

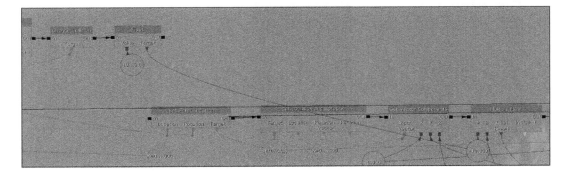

9. Remove the connection between the **Out** output of the **Set Vector Components** action to the **In** input of the **Set Actor Location** action. Select the **Level Loaded** event and the first **Set Vector Components** action connected to it along with the three float values by holding down *Ctrl + Alt*, and clicking to the top-left part of the **Level Loaded** event and dragging till you've selected everything.

10. Hold *Ctrl* and drag the event and actions away to add some room between the actions. Connect the **Out** output of the **Set Vector Components** action to the **In** input of the other **Set Vector Components** action, and the **Out** output of the **Change Collision** action to the **In** input of the **Set Actor Location** action. The new additions have been shifted to the top to make it easier to tell what is going on.

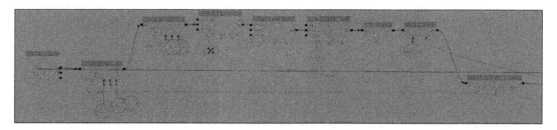

11. Back in the editor, select our asteroid and the emitter. Right-click on the objects and select the **Create Prefab...** option. In the dialog box that pops up, put in `Hotshot03` for the **Package** field and `AsteroidPrefab` for the **Name** field. After filling this out press the **OK** button. It will say that it found a sequence for the prefab. Say **Yes** to make the sequence part of the prefab, and **No** to make the object an instance of the prefab. As soon as this happens, go into the **Content Browser** window and save our **Hotshot03** package in the same folder as your level.

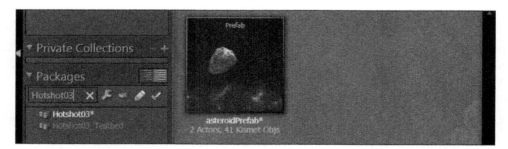

12. Create nine duplicates of your asteroid prefab by holding down the *Alt* key and dragging to a new location.

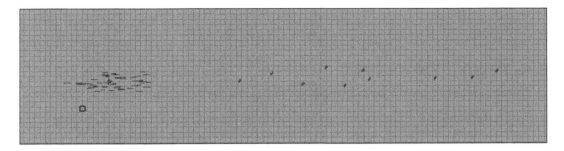

13. Save your project (**File | Save All**) and start your game by pressing *F8* or selecting **Play | In Editor** on the main toolbar.

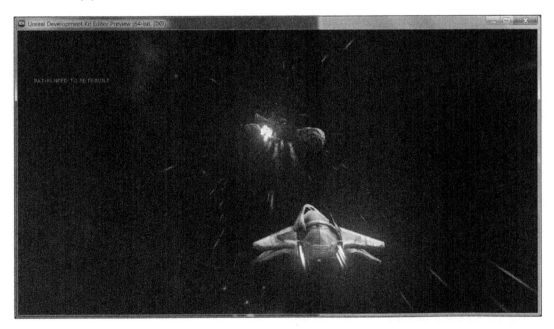

Objective Complete - Mini Debriefing

At this point our level is filled with many different asteroids for the player to avoid! Now we are on the right track to make this project more enjoyable!

Spawning enemies

Now that the player has asteroids to avoid, let's increase the difficulty by adding in enemies that can shoot at the player.

Engage Thrusters

Now let's start adding in enemies that can shoot at the player!

1. Import all of the files for the enemies located in the `Assets/Enemy` folder. Right-click in the same **Content Browser** window and select **New Material**. Inside the menu that pops up, confirm that the name **Hotshot03** is in the **Package** section and put in `EnemyMaterial` as the name of the file in the **Name** field.

2. Drag-and-drop the **enemy_diffuse**, **enemy_normal**, and **enemy_specular** textures and connect them to the appropriate slot as shown in the following screenshot. Click on the green checkmark and exit out of the Material Editor.

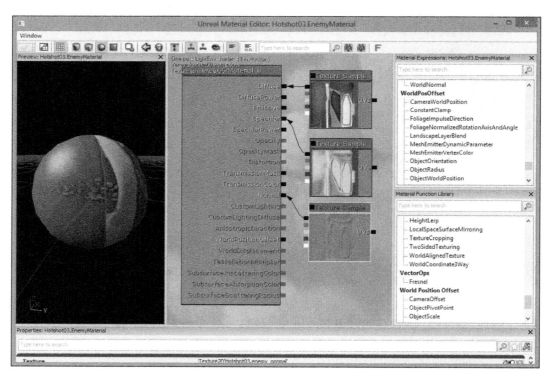

3. Back in the **Content Browser** window double-click on the new enemy ship mesh. Check off **Can Become Dynamic** and type in `material` in the Properties bar. Select **EnemyMaterial** in the **Content Browser** window by clicking on it, and click on the green arrow in order to set it as the material for the object. Create collision for the object by clicking on the **Collision | Auto Convex Collision** option. From there click on the **Apply** button and wait for it to generate collision data for us.

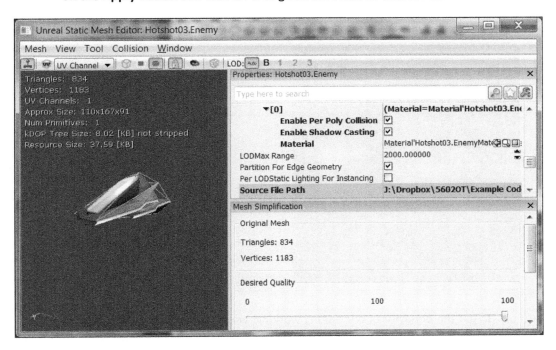

4. Exit the Static Mesh Editor. Back in the main editor add this new enemy ship into our level by right-clicking on our ship as a starting point and selecting **Add InterpActor : Hotshot03.EnemyShip**. Rotate the ship so that it is facing our player. In its Properties window change the **Collision Type** variable to **Collide_BlockAll**.

5. Place two dynamic PathNodes in front of it by duplicating them from the player, rotating them 180 degrees, and then selecting them both, selecting the lock icon and selecting the enemy ship as their base. Next, create an emitter with a particle system different from what we previously used, as we want an effect that is different when we destroy ships compared to the one used for asteroids. I personally used `ParticleSystem'WP_ShockRifle.Particles.P_WP_ShockRifle_Explo'`.

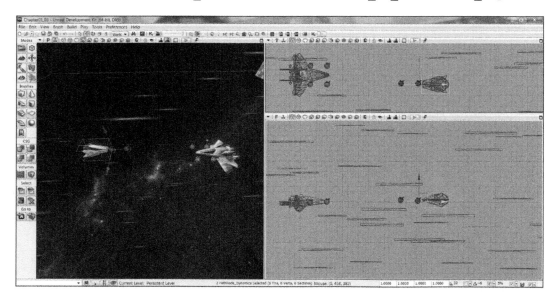

6. To get the behavior of our enemy working, we will need aspects from both the asteroid and the player with some custom nodes linking them both. We'll start doing that now.

7. Open up Kismet and create a new subsequence called **Enemy**. Create a **Level Loaded** event by right-clicking and selecting **New Event | Level Loaded**.

8. To the right-hand side of it, create a **Compare Bool** comparison by right-clicking and selecting **New Conditional | Comparison | Compare Bool**. Connect **Loaded** and **Visible** from the **Level Loaded** event to the **In** input of the **Compare Bool** comparison.

9. To the right-hand side of the **Compare Bool** action create two **Get Location and Rotation** actions. Connect the **True** output from the **Compare Bool** comparison to the **In** input of the first **Get Location and Rotation** action. Connect the **False** output of the **Compare Bool** action to the **In** input of the same action.

10. Right-click on the **In** input of the **Compare Bool** action and create a 0.2 delay by selecting **Set Activate Delay**. In the **Get Location and Rotation** action under the **Target** property, select the PathNode that is closest to the enemy's ship. Then, for the second **Get Location and Rotation** action, use the other node.

I inserted a short delay due to the fact that computers are extremely fast, and if I just connected a group of nodes together without any delay, something called an infinite loop may happen. This means that the code goes on forever without stopping, and as we want other things to happen in our project, we put in a delay.

11. Connect the **Out** output for the first **Get Location and Rotation** action to the **In** input of the second. To the right-hand side of both the **Get Location and Rotation** actions create a **Spawn Projectile** action by right-clicking and selecting **New Action | Spawn Projectile**. Under the **Projectile** class use UTProj_LinkPlasma.

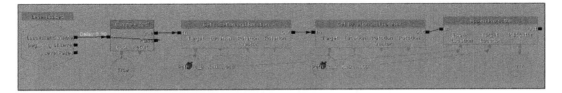

12. Next to the **Spawn Projectile** action create an **Add Int** action by right-clicking and selecting **New Action | Math | Add Int**. In the **B** section create an integer variable by right-clicking on it and selecting **Create New Int Variable**. In the Properties window change **Int Value** to 1. Create another integer variable with the value of 0 and connect it to both **A** and **IntResult**.

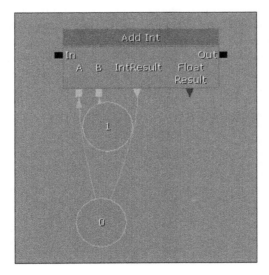

An **int**, also known as an **integer**, is a number without a decimal (floating) point part. I will use these terms interchangeably, because they mean the same thing. Inside Kismet they are a light-blue color.

13. Connect the **Out** output of the **Spawn Projectile** action to the **In** input of the **Add Int** action. Next to that, create a **Compare Int** comparison by right-clicking and selecting **New Conditional | Comparison | Compare Int**. In the **A** slot put the integer that we used in **A** and **IntResult** in the **Add Int** action. In the **B** slot create a new integer with a value of 5. Connect the **Out** output of the **Add Int** action to the **In** input of the **Compare Int** action. Connect the **A <= B** output from the **Compare Int** action to the **In** input of the **Compare Bool** action that we created in step 6.

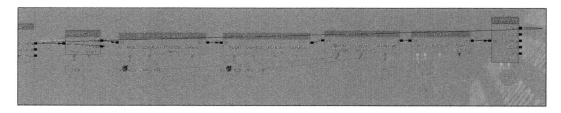

14. Next to that create a **Delay** action by right-clicking and selecting **New Action | Misc | Delay**. In the **Duration** section create a **Float** variable with a value of 2.0. Connect the **A > B** output from the **Compare Int** section to the **Start** input of the **Delay** action.

15. To the right-hand side of the **Delay** action create an **Int** action by right-clicking and selecting **New Action | Set Variable | Int**. Create a variable with the value of 0 for **Value** and connect to **Target** the same int that we've used for the **A** and **IntResult** slot of the **Add Int** action and the **A** slot of the **Compare Int** action. Connect **Finished** of the **Delay** action to the **In** input of the **Int** action. Connect the **Out** output of the **Int** action to the **In** input of the **Compare Bool** action that we created in step 6.

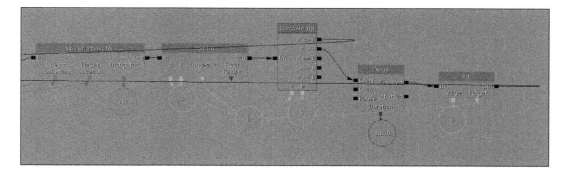

16. From one of the asteroid prefabs copy the **Touch** and **Take Damage** events from before. Paste it into our **Enemy** subsequence, changing the **InterpActor** values to the enemy ship's mesh, and the emitter to our enemy ship's emitter.

17. To the right-hand side of the **Change Collision** action create a **Toggle** action. Connect the **Out** output from the **Change Collision** action to the **Turn Off** input of the **Toggle** action. Connect **Bool** in the **Toggle** action to **Bool** that we created in step 6.

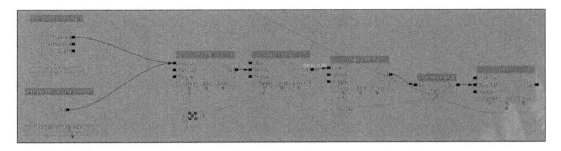

18. Now go back to the asteroid prefabs and copy (*Ctrl + C*) and paste (*Ctrl + V*) the **Level Loaded** event that moved the asteroid and everything that it entailed, changing the **InterpActor** values to the enemy ship mesh and the emitter to our enemy ship's emitter.

19. Remove the second **Set Vector Components** action that created the rotation for the asteroid, and in its place create a **Bool** action by right-clicking and selecting **New Action | Set Variable | Bool**. In the **Value** section create **Bool** with a value of 1 (True). For **Target**, connect it to the same **Bool** that we are referencing from step 6. Connect the **Out** output from the first **Set Vector Components** action to the **In** input of the **Bool** action.

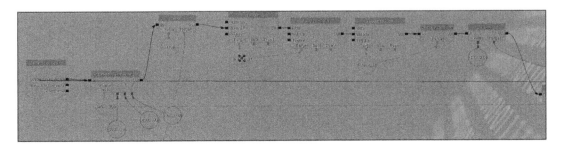

20. Save your project (**File** | **Save All**) and start your game by pressing *F8* or selecting **Play** | **In Editor** on the main toolbar.

Objective Complete - Mini Debriefing

With the help of the things that we've already created, we have used little pieces from here and there to create a unique object that can fire at us for short periods and can shoot asteroids as well. At this point, we could create a prefab of the object to have as many ships as we want, but I feel that the sight of a ship once in a while is much more impressive than a bunch flying around.

Opening cutscene

To really reinforce the fact that we are moving through space, it may be a good idea to have an opening cutscene.

Engage Thrusters

That being said, let's create our opening cutscene!

1. Just in case you haven't done so already, first select all of the asteroids that you have in the level and arrange them in a random position and rotation.

2. Select one of the emitters by right-clicking and selecting **Select | Select All Emitter Actors**, then press *F4* to access the emitters' properties. Uncheck **Auto Activate**.

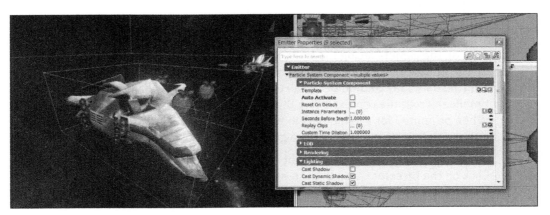

3. Go to the **ActorClasses** tab and click on the **CameraActor** panel and place it in our level. Rotate the camera so that it faces our ship directly. Duplicate it and create another camera that faces our ship from the other side.

4. Go into Kismet and create another **Level Loaded** event by right-clicking and selecting **New Event | Level Loaded**. To the right-hand side of it create a new **Matinee** sequence by right-clicking and selecting **New Matinee**. Connect **Loaded** and **Visible** from the **Level Loaded** event to **Play** of the **Matinee** sequence.

5. Click on the camera facing the front of the ship inside the editor, then double-click on the **Matinee** sequence to enter the Matinee Editor. Right-click inside the Group List (the dark-gray column below all the tabs with text and that is to the left of the timeline). From the context menu that appears, click on **Add New Camera Group**. When prompted for a name type in `BackCamera`. Likewise, after that select the side camera and create another camera group with the name `SideCamera`.

6. Create a new director group by right-clicking and selecting **Add New Director Group**. Click on the **Director** track, then create a keyframe 2 seconds after the beginning of the **Matinee** sequence and select **BackCamera** as the camera to use.

 To get an exact time for a keyframe within the Matinee Editor, you may right-click on it and select **Set Time** and put in whatever time you want.

7. Create another keyframe at the 2.5 second mark and use the **SideCamera** as the camera to use. Create another keyframe at the 5.0 second mark that is going to **DirGroup** in order to return the control back to the normal camera. Right-click on the **SideCamera** keyframe and select **Set Transition Time** and set it with a value of 2.0. Right-click on the **DirGroup** keyframe and use **Set Transition Time** of 3.0.

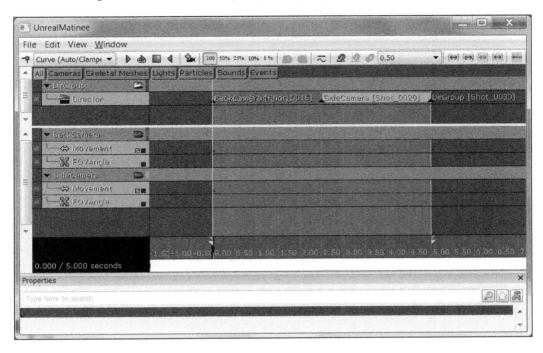

8. Close the Matinee Editor and confirm that both cameras are attached to the **Matinee** sequence and are appropriately slotted.

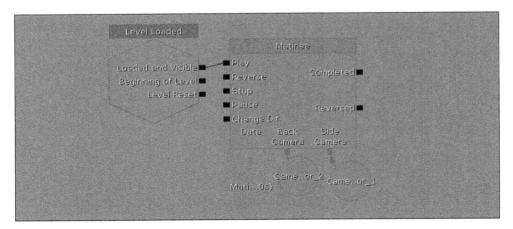

9. Click on the player's ship and go back into the Matinee Editor and create a new **CameraGroup** variable with it and a **Group Name** value of Ship. Create keyframes at 0.0, at 0.01, and at 2.5. Translate the ship far away along the y axis on the 0.01 keyframe, keeping the other two keyframes unchanged.

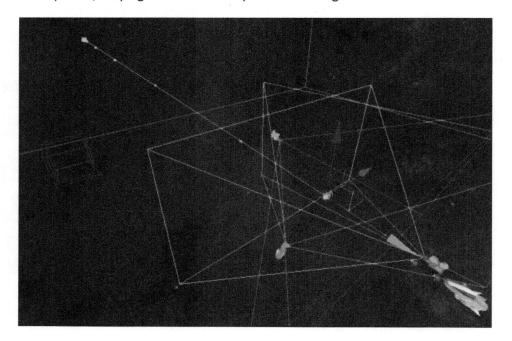

10. Create another keyframe slightly after that so there is not much movement, then move that key over to 2.0 by holding *Ctrl* and dragging it over or by right-clicking and selecting **Set Time**.

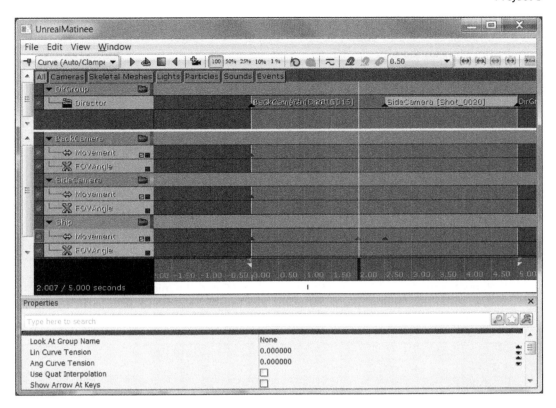

11. Exit out of the Matinee Editor and create a **Float** action by right-clicking and selecting **New Action | Set Variable | Float**. In the **Value** section put in a new **Float** variable by right-clicking and selecting **Create New Float Variable** and put the value of 1.0 inside it. In the **Target** section create a named variable by right-clicking and selecting **New Variable | Named Variable**. In **Find Var Name** put in Speed and you should see the green checkmark come up. Connect the **Out** output from the **Matinee** sequence to the **In** input of the **Float** action with a 2.0 second activation delay.

12. To the right-hand side of the **Float** action create a **Toggle** action by right-clicking and selecting **New Action | Toggle | Toggle**. In the **Target** section put the two top thrusters on the player's ship.

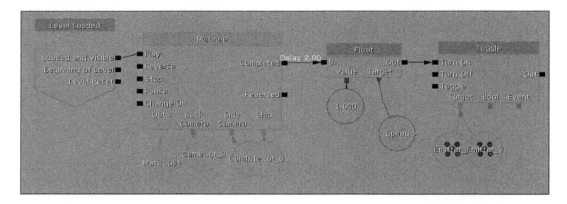

13. Repeat steps 11 and 12 using the values **3** and **5** and the middle row and bottom row of the thrusters respectively. In the last **Toggle** action, also include the **Speed** emitter that we created in the last project and a delay of only 1.0 second.

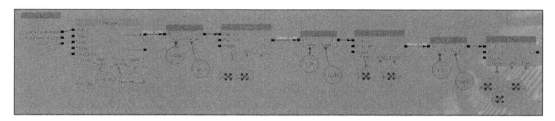

14. Build your project by selecting **Build | Build All**. Save your game using **File | Save All** and run the game by selecting **Play | In Editor**.

Objective Complete - Mini Debriefing

What an exciting opening! Our hero comes in from some kind of space, jumps into this asteroid field while having to clear the area out manually with particles turning on, giving the illusion of speed in a very effective manner. It would be difficult for people to think that it was everything else and not the player that was moving, and yet, that is exactly what we have done.

Player's health/HUD

Now that we have our player figured out and basic gameplay implemented, let's take some time to add in a way for the player to gauge how well he is doing.

Engage Thrusters

With that, let's create a rudimentary HUD using just Kismet and a few static meshes.

1. Create a duplicate of our player ship by holding down the *Alt* key and dragging it upwards. Press *F4* to bring up its Properties menu. Search for the `Scale` property and give it a value of `0.25` and change the **Location** value in the **X** property to `400`. In the **Y** property put `0`, and in **Z** put `375`. Change the **Physics** type to `PHYS_Rotating` and change **Rotation Rate** to have `60` for the **Yaw** value. Under **Display** check off the **Hidden** option. Let the base of the ship be the normal camera. Type `Depth` into the search bar and change the **Depth Priority Group** value of the object to `SDPG_Foreground`.

> The Depth Priority Group is a feature that is rarely used even by experienced users of Unreal, so I thought it would be a good idea to mention it. It basically tells the engine in what order to draw things. Putting the ships into the foreground means that they will be drawn on top of everything else in the game, just like an HUD in a normal game. You can do a lot of things with this, such as create thermal vision or the "Detective Mode" within Rocksteady's Batman games, *Arkham Asylum* and *Arkham City*, which allow you to see enemies through walls.

2. Create two copies of the new ship by holding down the *Alt* key and dragging along the x axis towards the ship, leaving room between copies for the ships to rotate around.

3. Go into the **Content Browser** window and find an explosion that you want to use on the player's ship to create a lot of damage. I personally used `ParticleSystem'FX_ VehicleExplosions.Effects.P_FX_VehicleDeathExplosion'`. Inside its properties, change the **Scale** value to 3 and make the ship as the emitter's base and uncheck the **Auto Activate** property.

4. Open up Kismet and go to the **Level Loaded** event with the **Matinee** sequence that we created in the previous section. Next to the final **Toggle** action we created, create a **Toggle Hidden** action by right-clicking and selecting **New Action | Toggle | Toggle Hidden**.

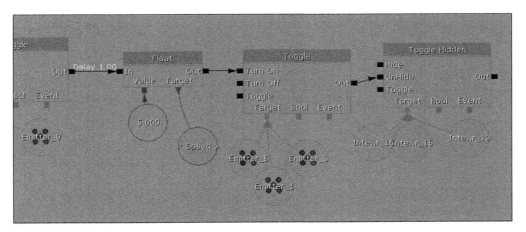

5. Go to the **Touch** event of the player's ship that we created in the previous project. Create a **Take Damage** event for that ship by clicking on the ship in the editor, right-clicking, and selecting **New Event Using InterpActor_12 | Take Damage**. Connect the **Out** output from it to the **Play** input of the **Play CameraAnim** action.

6. To the right-hand side of the **Play CameraAnim** action, create an **Activate Remote Event** action by right-clicking and selecting **New Action | Event | Activate Remote Event**. Under **Event Name** put in the value `PlayerDamaged`. Connect the **Out** output of the **Play CameraAnim** action to the **In** input of the **Activate Remote Event** action.

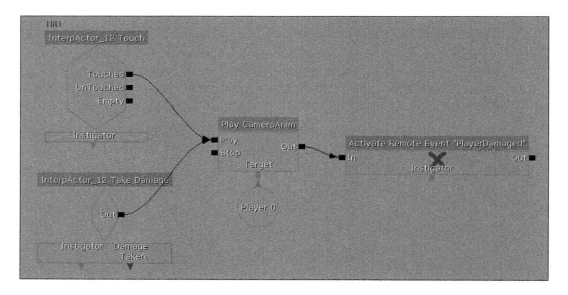

7. Move your Kismet window to an area with a large space and create an integer variable with the name of `Lives` and **Int Value** of 3.

8. Underneath that, create **Remote Event** by right-clicking and selecting **New Event | Remote Event**. In the **Event Name** section, put `PlayerDamaged` and press *Enter*; you should see a green checkmark that will replace the red X there.

9. To the right-hand side of **Remove Event**, create a **Subtract Int** action by right-clicking and selecting **New Action | Math | Subtract Int**. In the **A** and **IntResult** spots create a named variable that uses the **Lives** integer variable. In the **B** spot create an integer with the value of 1. Connect the **Out** output of **Remote Event 'Player Damaged'** to the **In** input of the **Subtract Int** action.

10. To the right-hand side of that, create a **Compare Int** comparison by right-clicking and selecting **New Condition | Comparison | Compare Int**. In the **A** slot create another **Named Variable** with **Lives**, and in **B** put the value 2 (one less than the maximum amount of lives). Connect the **Out** output of the **Subtract Int** action to the **In** input of the **Compare Int** comparison.

11. After that, create a **Toggle Hidden** action. For **Target**, go into the editor, click on the ship that is furthest to the left, then return to Kismet and create an object variable using it. Connect the **A == B** output to the **Hide** input of the **Toggle Hidden** action.

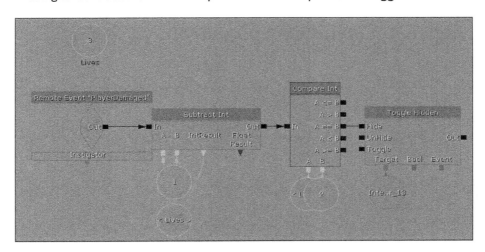

12. Copy and paste the **Compare Int** and **Toggle Hidden** actions and position them below and to the right-hand side of the already existing ones. Change the **B** slot of this newly created **Compare Int** to 1. Change **Target** of the new **Toggle Hidden** action to the middle ship. Connect the **A < B** output to the **In** input of the new **Compare Int** action.

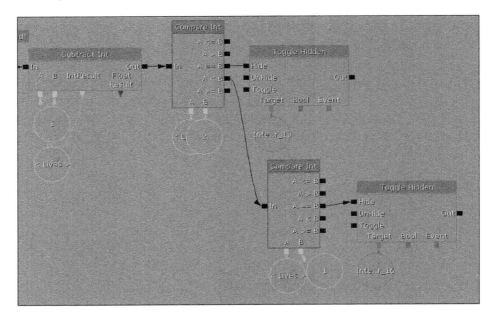

13. Do this one last time for the **0** case with the other ship in the same manner as the previous step, connecting the **A < B** output to the **In** input of the new **Compare Int** action.

14. Below that and to the right-hand side, create a **Toggle** action. In the **Target** section find the player's ship explosion emitter that we created in step 3 and use it. Connect the **A < B** output of the **0** case **Compare Int** action to the **Turn On** input of this **Toggle** action.

15. To the right-hand side of that, create another **Toggle** action. In the **Target** section put all of the seven emitters used by the player, that is, the **speed** emitter and the six jets. Connect the **Event** section to all of the **Key/Button Pressed** events (the Space bar for shooting and movement). Connect the **Out** output from the first **Toggle** action to the **Turn Off** input of this **Toggle** action.

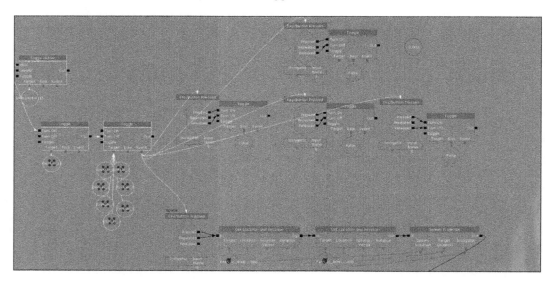

16. After that, create a **Toggle Hidden** event with the player's ship as **Target**. Connect the **Out** output from the **Toggle** action to the **In** input of the **Toggle Hidden** action.

17. To the right-hand side of that action, create a **Change Collision** action by right-clicking and selecting **New Action | Actor | Change Collision**. In the Properties window change the **Collision Type** variable to **COLLIDE_NoCollision**. Connect the **Target** section to the player's ship, similar to what we did in the previous step, and connect the **Out** output from the **Toggle Hidden** action to the **In** input of the **Change Collision** action.

18. Finally, create a **Console Command** action by right-clicking and selecting **New Action | Misc | Console Command**. In the **Commands[0]** variable type in `quit`. Under **Target**, create a **Player 0** variable by right-clicking and selecting **New Variable | Player | Player**, and in the Properties window, by unchecking the **All Players** option. Connect the **Out** output from the **Change Collision** action to the **In** input of the **Console Command** action.

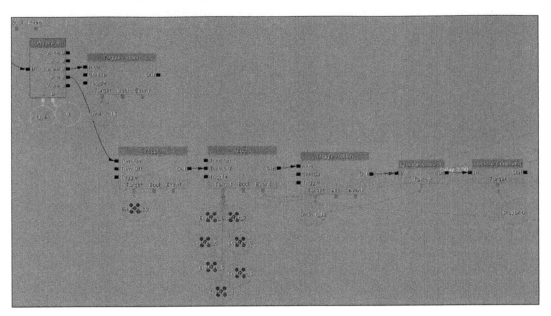

19. Build your project by selecting **Build | Build All**. Save your game using **File | Save All** and run the game by selecting **Play | In Editor**.

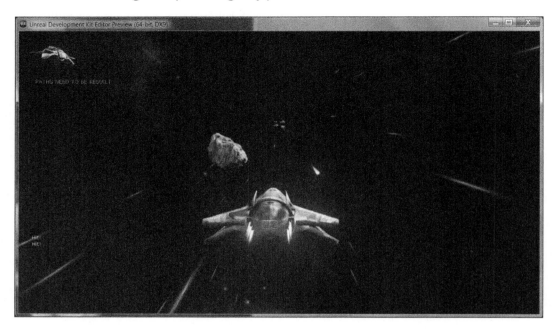

Objective Complete - Mini Debriefing

At this point, we finally have an ending to our game and a way to gauge a player's progress within the game through the implementation of a health system. We have also implemented a rudimentary HUD for players to know exactly when they lost their health and how careful they must be from this point. We have also created a Game Over state, which will destroy the player's ship and quit the game for us until the player wants to play again.

Mission Accomplished

Taking a little more time on a project can definitely make a project much more polished, and it certainly shows in this project. We took some time to change our single asteroid into a prefab, thereby making it very easy for us to create a large number of them to populate our world. We then created an enemy, which will travel in pretty much the same way as the asteroids, apart from the fact that the enemies shoot at the player. The player will also have an ample amount of time where they can fight with the enemies without damaging themselves.

Speaking of damage, we also added health to the player, only allowing them to make so many mistakes before the game ends with the player's ship being destroyed due to it being hit too much, for which we created a visual feedback by creating a rudimentary HUD system. Let's take one final look at what we have accomplished:

You Ready to go Gung HO? A Hotshot Challenge

Through this project we have learned how to do a lot more to polish our project within a short period of time, but there are still plenty of things we can do! How about you take some time between projects and try to complete the following:

 ▸ Have enemies attempt to move towards the player as they travel (Hint: the **Trace** action will help).

 ▸ When a player gets hit, give them invincibility for a short period of time before they can get hit again.

 ▸ Add new emitters to change the ship as it gets damaged, such as adding smoke and/or making the jets toggle on and off to show the ship in various states of damage.

 ▸ Add a score variable that will increment every time we destroy a ship or asteroid. Once we learn how to use Scaleform, go back and replace our rudimentary HUD with one of your own creation.

 ▸ Add a health pickup that will have the player regain health back and adjust Kismet to allow for that with a **PlayerHealed** remote event.

Project 4

Creating a
Custom HUD

We can have the most fun game in the world, but if the player has no idea what's going on it is next to impossible for that fun to be experienced by anyone other than the creator. One of the main tools that we use within the game industry to pass on information to the user is a heads-up display, more commonly referred to as a HUD.

The tool that most modern-day games use for doing user-interface (UI) work, such as HUDs, is **Scaleform**. Scaleform has been used with great success in Unreal games such as *Borderlands 2*, *Mass Effect 3*, *XCOM: Enemy Unknown*, and *Bioshock Infinite*.

Scaleform allows users to bring in Flash animation files to UDK to be rendered directly on the screen or rendered onto textures that can be used within the game world. We can interact with these movies using both Kismet and UnrealScript to create whatever kind of interface you can dream of.

We implemented a very simplistic version of a HUD in *Project 3*, *Terror in Deep Space: Even Deeper*, but in this project we're going to dive right in to creating our own HUD from scratch to be used in a Medieval RPG.

Mission Briefing

In this project we will be creating a HUD that can be used within a Medieval RPG and that will fit nicely into the provided Epic Citadel map, making use of Scaleform and ActionScript 3.0 using Adobe Flash CS6.

Why Is It Awesome?

At the end of this project, we will have created the basis of a heads-up display, making use of Scaleform, importing a project from Flash, and we will touch on how to communicate between UDK and Flash. The HUD will adjust based on the health a player has, and this can easily be expanded upon for your own personal projects.

Your Hotshot Objectives

As usual, we will be following a simple step-by-step process from beginning to end to complete the project. Here is the outline of our tasks:

- ► Setting up Flash
- ► Creating our HUD
- ► Importing Flash files into UDK

Mission Checklist

Scaleform does not require us to use Adobe Flash, but that is the environment we will be using to create our UI content. I will be using the latest Adobe Flash CS6, but it is possible to do most of the things in this project using the previous version. For those without Flash, Adobe offers a free trial of all their software. For more information on that, please visit `www.adobe.com/go/tryflash/`.

We will also need the art assets for our menu. These can be downloaded from the support page on Packt Publishing's website, at `www.packtpub.com/support`.

Setting up Flash

Our first step will be setting up Flash in order for us to create our HUD. In order to do this, we must first install the Scaleform Launcher.

Prepare for Lift Off

At this point, I will assume that you have run Adobe Flash CS6 at least once beforehand. If not, you can skip this section to where we actually import the `.swf` file into UDK. Alternatively, you can try to use some other way to create a Flash animation, such as FlashDevelop, Flash Builder, or SlickEdit; but that will have to be done on your own.

Engage Thrusters

The first step will be to install the Scaleform Launcher. The launcher will make it very easy for us to test our Flash content using the GFX hardware-accelerated Flash Player, which is what UDK will use to play it. Let's get started.

1. Open up Adobe Flash CS6 Professional. Once the program starts up, open up **Adobe Extension Manager** by going to **Help | Manage Extensions...**.

You may see the menu say **Performing configuration tasks, please wait...**. This is normal; just wait for it to bring up the menu as shown in the following screenshot:

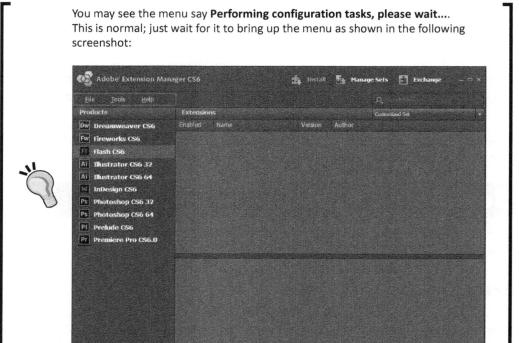

2. Click on the **Install** option from the top menu on the right-hand side of the screen. In the file browser, locate the path of your UDK installation and then go into the `Binaries\GFx\CLICK Tools\` folder. Once there, select the `ScaleformExtensions.mxp` file and then select **OK**.

3. When the agreement comes up, press the **Accept** button; then select whether you want the program to be installed for just you or everyone on your computer.

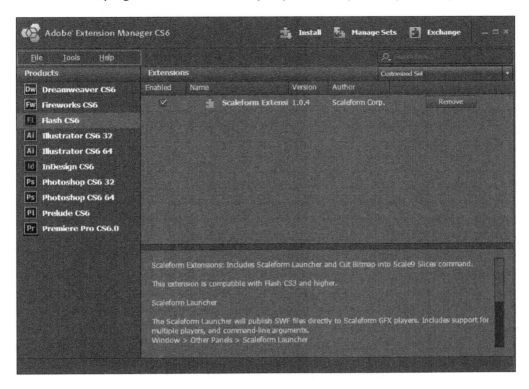

4. If Flash is currently running, you should get a window popping up telling you that the program will not be ready until you restart the program. Close the manager and restart the program.

5. With your reopened version of Flash start up the Scaleform Launcher by clicking on **Window | Other Panels | Scaleform Launcher**.

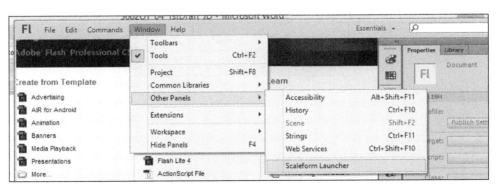

6. At this point you should see the **Scaleform Launcher** panel come up as shown in the following screenshot:

7. At this point all of the options are grayed out as it doesn't know how to access the GFx player, so let's set that up now.

8. Click on the **+** button to add a new profile. In the **profile name** section, type in `GFXMediaPlayer`. Next, we need to reference the GFx player. Click on the **+** button in the **player EXE** section. Go to your UDK directory, `Binaries\GFx\`, and then select `GFxMediaPlayerD3d9.exe`. It will then ask you to give a name for the **Player Name** field with the value already filled in; just hit the **OK** button.

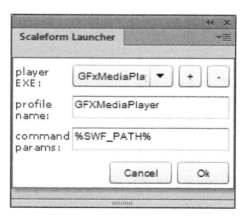

UDK by default uses DirectX 9 for rendering. However, since GDC 2011, it has been possible for users to use DirectX 11. If your project is using 11, feel free to check out `http://udn.epicgames.com/Three/DirectX11Rendering.html` and use DX11.

9. In order to test our game, we will need to hit the button that says **Test with: GFxMediaPlayerD3d9** as shown in the following screenshot:

 If you know the resolution in which you want your final game to be, you can set up multiple profiles to preview how your UI will look at a specific resolution. For example, if you'd like to see something at a resolution of 960 x 720, you can do so by altering the **command params** field after `%SWF PATH%` to include the text `-res 960:720`.

10. Now that we have the player loaded, we need to install the CLIK library for our usage. Go to the **Preferences** menu by selecting **Edit | Preferences**. Click on the **ActionScript** tab and then click on the **ActionScript 3.0 Settings...** button.

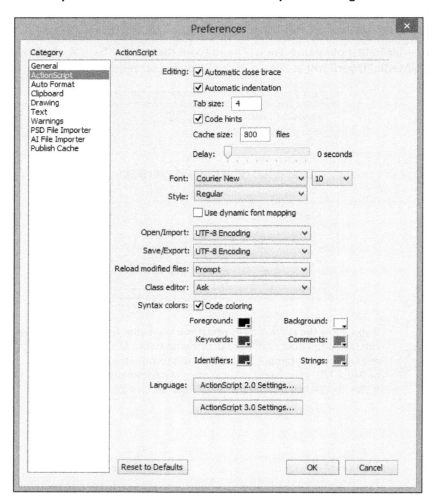

11. From there, add a new entry to our **Source path** section by clicking on the **+**
button. After that, click on the folder icon to browse to the folder we want. Add an
additional path to our CLIK directory in the file explorer by first going to your UDK
installation directory and then going to Development\Flash\AS3\CLIK.

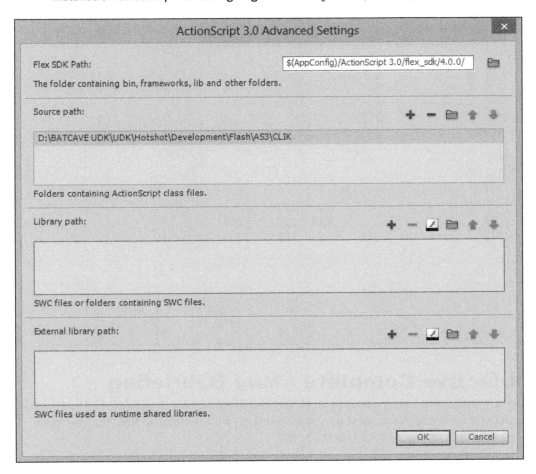

12. Click on the **OK** button and drag-and-drop the newly created Scaleform Launcher to the bottom-right corner of the interface.

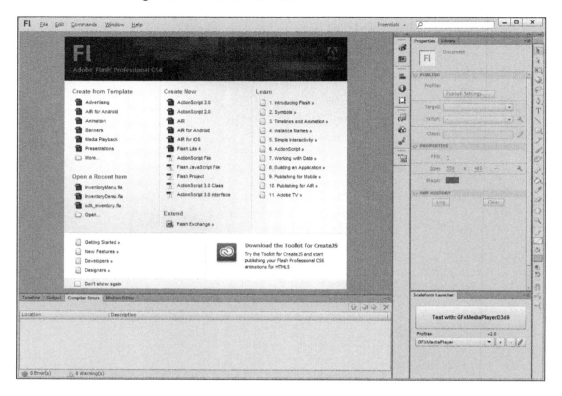

Objective Complete - Mini Debriefing

Alright, Flash is now set up for us to work with Scaleform within it, which for all intents and purposes is probably the hardest part about working with Scaleform. Now that we have taken care of it, let's get started on the HUD!

As long as you have administrator access to your computer, these settings should be set for whenever you are working with Flash. However, if you do not, you will have to run through all of these settings every time you want to work on Scaleform projects.

Creating our HUD

Now that Flash is set up, let's actually create our HUD menu.

Prepare for Lift Off

But before we get into that, let's talk a little bit about the environment, as I'm guessing many of you may never have worked with Flash before.

Flash 101: an introduction

As you begin your project, there may be many new panels and areas that are yours to use.

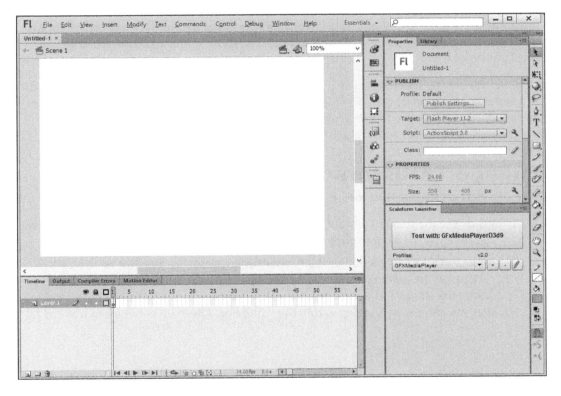

Stage

The largest area in the top-left section is called the stage. This is where all of the action within our menus will take place. Users will only see the white-box area of the stage and the objects that are in it.

Properties inspector

The **Properties** area is to the right-hand side of the stage. In much the same way as UDK has properties for all of its actors, Flash allows us to change the variables associated with our objects. When nothing else is selected, by default the **Properties** inspector shows properties that we can change about the stage, such as the size, FPS (frames per second), and background color.

Tools panel

On the far right is the Tools panel. These are basic tools that you can use to draw and create basic shapes while also moving objects around. Each of these objects has a specific use; it is a good idea to play around with it on your own.

Timeline

The area on the bottom of the screen is known as the **Timeline**. Here we can use keyframes and layers to create animation with different objects. Those familiar with Matinee will be very familiar with this.

Now, we will only be touching Flash in a way to get the UI completed, but Flash itself could be a series of books on its own. For the adventurous, some links that I used when I was just starting out with Flash are `http://www.kirupa.com/developer/flash/index.htm` and the not-updated-but-still-useful `http://active.tutsplus.com/`.

Engage Thrusters

Now let's start create our HUD menu!

1. Inside the main menu of Adobe Flash, create a new ActionScript 3.0 project by going to **Create New | ActionScript 3.0**.

2. In the **PROPERTIES** section of the **Properties** inspector, set the **Size** to `1280 x 720` by clicking on the existing numbers and typing in the new values and then hitting *Enter*. Above the stage, find the zoom scaling that currently says **100%** and change it so that you can see everything within the white box. Alternatively, you can use *Ctrl + 1*.

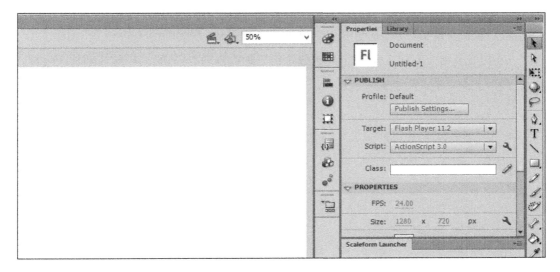

3. Access the **Library** section by clicking on the tab next to the **Properties** tab. Outside of Flash, go to the project's `assets` folder.

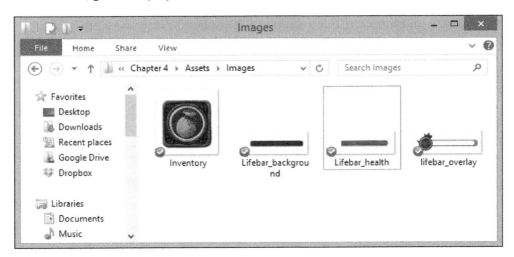

4. Select all of the files and drag-and-drop them into the **Library** tab. Wait for the import dialog to finish and you should see all of the files placed there.

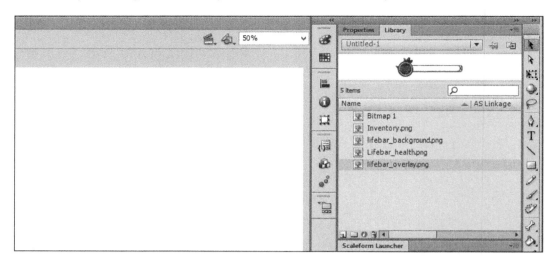

5. From there, go to the **Timeline** section at the bottom of the screen and create a new layer by either clicking on the new layer button at the very bottom-left corner of the program or by right-clicking on **Layer1** and selecting **New Layer**. Double-click on the layer on the top and change its name to `ActionScript`. Double-click on the other layer and give it the name of `Lifebar`. Create two more layers, one above the **Lifebar** layer with the name of `Overlay` and one below with the name of `Background`. You can drag-and-drop layers to put them where you want them.

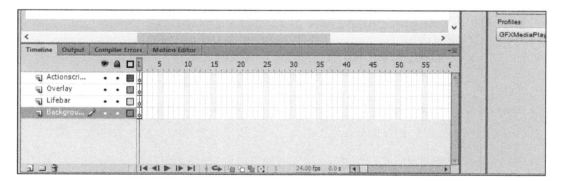

6. Click on the first keyframe of the **Background** layer. Drag-and-drop the `Lifebar_background.png` image to the top-left corner of the stage.

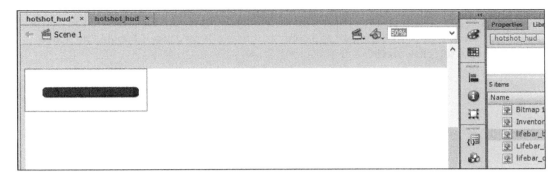

7. Continue to place the `Lifebar_overlay.png` file in the **Overlay** layer and the `Lifebar_health.png` file into the **Lifebar** layer between them.

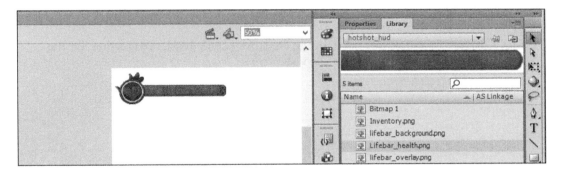

8. Now, we won't be touching the overlay or backgrounds anymore, so on both of those layers click on the dots under the little lock for those layers, to lock them so that we can't change it anymore. You can notice where to click and where the locks are in the following screenshot:

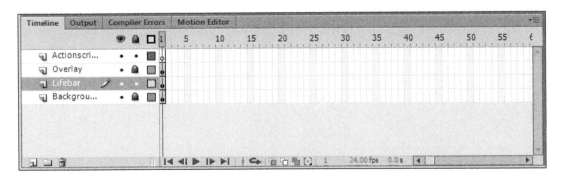

9. Next, in order to reference our lifebar in code, we need to have some way to reference it. In order to do that, we're going to have to make our graphic into a movie clip. Thankfully, it's very easy. Click to select and then right-click on the `lifebar` object and select **Convert to Symbol...** (or press *F8*). There, in the **Name** section, type in `lifebarMC` and confirm that the **Type** value is **Movie Clip**. Once that is set, click on **OK**.

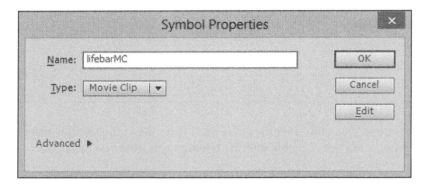

10. Click on the **Properties** tab with the lifebar selected. In the textbox that has the instance's name in it, change the value to `lifebar`.

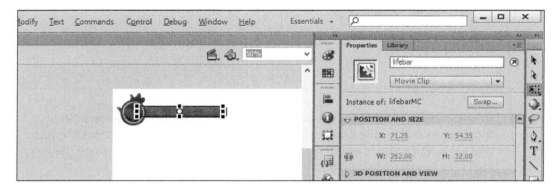

11. Click on the **Lifebar** layer and then click on our health image. Then select the Free Transform tool by either clicking on the third icon on the Tools panel or by pressing the Q key (the icon selected in the following screenshot on the far right). You should see a white circle in the middle of our image; this is the point at which scaling will begin. Click and drag that circle to the far left of the image on the x axis and to the middle of the image on the y axis.

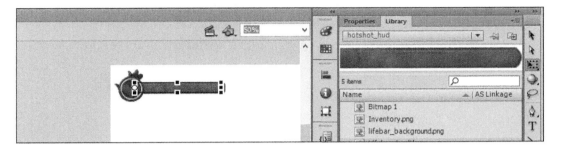

 If you'd like to see how scaling changes depending on where the white dot is, press *Ctrl + T* to open up the transform tool and change the value of the **X** scaling. Just make sure it's set to 100 before you move to the next step.

12. Save your project by going to **File | Save**, and type in a name of your choice (I used hotshot_hud). Click on the stage once again and access the **Properties** inspector. Under **Publish** in **Class**, type in the same name (hotshot_hud). Afterwards, click on the pencil beside it and you should see the following warning:

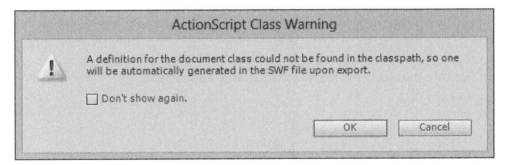

13. Click on the **Test with: GFxMediaPlayerD3d9** button to start up our program. After it has run, close it along with the console window that opened up with it. Click on the pencil icon again and it may ask what to open with. Select **Flash Professional** and click **OK**. You should see some code in the pop-up window already written for us. Save that file (by hitting *Ctrl + S*) with the filename given to you, in the same folder as the `.fla` file (hotshot_hud).

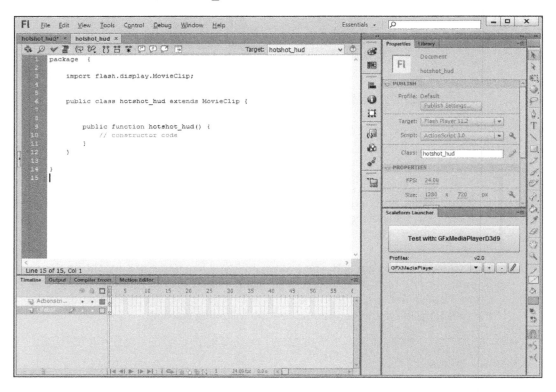

14. Replace the text in the file with the following code snippet:

```
package  {

    // Needed for the stage
    importflash.display.MovieClip;

    // Allows us to use Scaleform
    importscaleform.gfx.Extensions;

    //Allows us to use the Event.ENTER_FRAME event listener
```

```
import flash.events.Event;

// Declaring the Document class
public class hotshot_hud extends MovieClip
{
    // Variables that we will be using to show the
    // player's current and max health
    public static var currentHealth:int = 100;
    public static var maxHealth:int = 100;

//Constructor will be called the first frame of the game
    public function hotshot_hud()
    {
        // Enables Scaleform
        Extensions.enabled = true;

        // Adds an event so that the Update function will
        // be called every single frame.
        addEventListener(Event.ENTER_FRAME,this.Update);
    }

    // Code that we want to run every frame of the game
    function Update(event:Event)
    {
        // Update our life's scale to reflect the current
        // ratio of currentHealth to maxHealth
        lifebar.scaleX = currentHealth/maxHealth;
    }
}

}
```

15. Save your project by hitting *Ctrl + S* on both files and then click on the **Test with: GFxMediaPlayerD3d9** button on the Scaleform Launcher to start up our program.

Objective Complete - Mini Debriefing

In a very simple way, we have created a good-looking HUD within Flash that we will be using in UDK with a few short steps!

Importing Flash files into UDK

Now that we have our content, let's bring it in!

Engage Thrusters

Let's now start importing Flash files into UDK.

1. UDK can only import Flash files that are within a specific folder. Inside your file browser, go to the folder with your `.fla` and `.as` files. In that folder, you should see a file with a `.swf` extension. Copy that file and go to your UDK installation folder (`UDKGame\Flash\`) and create a new folder called `Hotshot`. Inside that folder, paste the `.swf` Flash movie file.

 You must put Flash files within the `UDKGame\Flash\` folder or a subfolder of that folder. You can name the subfolder however you'd like.

2. Start up UDK again. Open up the **Content Browser** window and click on the **Import** button. Find the movie file and click **OK**. You will notice that the **Import** dialog already sets the package name to **Hotshot**, so just say **OK** and save this package.

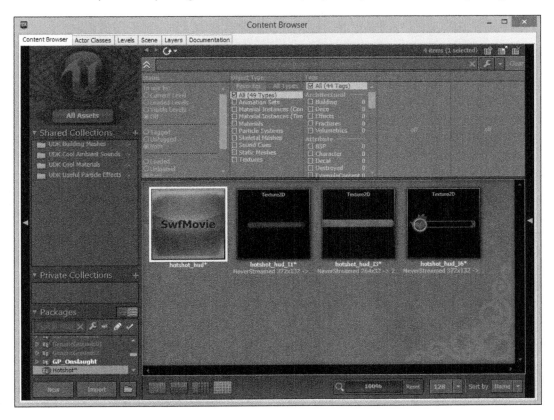

3. With the movie selected, open up Kismet. Create a **Level Loaded** event by right-clicking and going to **New Event** | **Level Loaded**.

4. To the right-hand side of that, create an **Open GFx Movie** action by right-clicking and gong to **New Action | GFx UI | Open GFx Movie**. Connect the **Loaded** and **Visible** outputs from the **Level Loaded** event to the **In** input of the **Open GFx Movie** action.

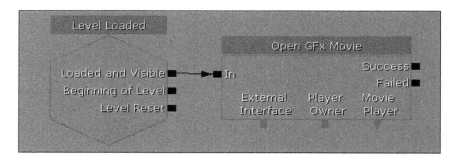

5. Create a player variable for **Player Owner** by right-clicking and going to **New Variable | Player | Player**, and in the Properties window uncheck the **All Players** option.

6. Create a new object variable for **Movie Player** by right-clicking on the pink arrow and selecting **Create New Object Variable**.

7. Go back into the **Content Browser** window and select the SwfMovie that we imported previously. Back in Kismet, click on the **Open GFx Movie** action to see its properties; and click on the green arrow in the **Movie** property to see the value `SwfMovie'Hotshot.hotshot_hud'` be filled in.

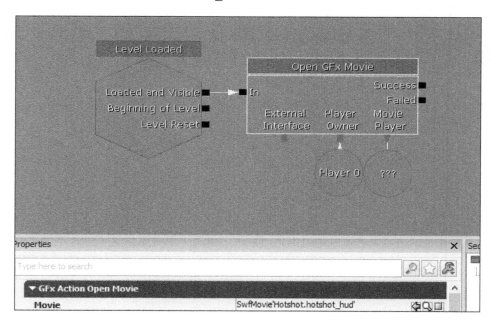

8. Next, create a **Get Property** action by right-clicking and going to **New Action |
    Object Property | Get Property**. Under the **Target** section, create another **Player
    0** variable. In the **Int** section, create a new integer variable. Click on the action to
    access its properties. Under **Property Name**, type `Health`. Connect the **Success**
    output of the **Open GFx Movie** action to the **In** input of the **Get Property** action.
    Create a delay of 0.2 seconds in the connect by right-clicking on the black square on
    the **In** input of the **Get Property** action and selecting **Set Activate Delay**.

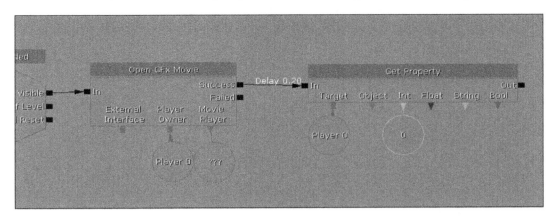

9. To the right-hand side of that, create a **GFx SetVariable** action by right-clicking
    and going to **New Action | GFx UI | GFx SetVariable**. Connect the **Value** section
    to the **Int** section we created in the **Get Property** action and the **Movie Player**
    section of the **GFx SetVariable** action to the **Movie Player** section of the **Open GFx
    Movie** action. In the action's properties, set the **Variable** value to `hotshot_hud.
    currentHealth`. Connect the **Out** output of the **Get Property** action to the **In** input
    of the **GFx SetVariable** action. Then connect the **Out** output of the **GFx SetVariable**
    action to the **In** input of the **Get Property** action.

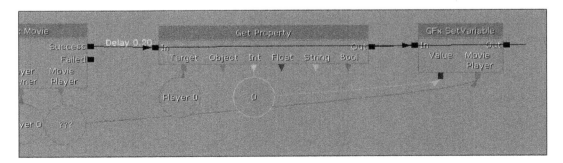

For a view of the entire Kismet sequence, please look at the following screenshot:

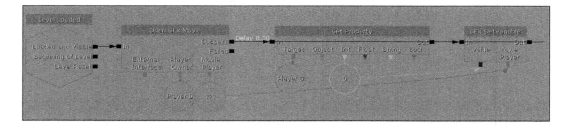

10. Build your project by going to **Build | Build All**. Save your game by going to **File | Save All**, and run our game by going to **Play | In Editor**.

Objective Complete - Mini Debriefing

And with that, our HUD is now fully functional. As our player gains and loses health, the HUD will coincide with that value. Dropping the Kismet we created into a level will work when the HUD's visuals make a lot of sense.

Or not...but it still works perfectly.

Mission Accomplished

One can clearly see after this mission how useful having Scaleform is and how powerful a tool it can be. Specifically, we just set Flash up so that we could implement something using Scaleform by adding the Scaleform Launcher to Flash, and imported the Scaleform libraries for our use. After that, we imported custom art assets into Flash and created a `Document` class to hold our code, which will update our health in every frame. Once we published our project, we went back into UDK and imported the file into a level and added Kismet to load the movie and use it as our main HUD, giving us a much more polished HUD than we created previously. Also, it gave you a taste of what can be done using Scaleform, which can be easily expanded upon. Let's take one final look at what we have accomplished:

You Ready to go Gung HO? A Hotshot Challenge

Through this project, we have learned how to create a HUD within a short period of time, but there is still plenty of things we can do! How about you take some time between projects and try to complete the following:

▶ Spend time learning about Scaleform and the features it has, at
  `http://udn.epicgames.com/Three/Scaleform.html`

▶ Use Scaleform to create HUDs for the previous projects that we've created

▶ Learn about Color Transforms (`http://www.republicofcode.com/tutorials/flash/as3colortransform/`) and create an HUD whose color changes to red if the player's health is less than 0.5

Project 5
Creating Environments

Sid Meier (famous for the *Civilization* series of games and Creative Director on *XCOM: Enemy Unknown*) claims that, "A game is a series of interesting choices." When video games were first created, people playing games used the game's mechanics to do different things without much concern about the world the game took place in. However, as games became more sophisticated and stories kept getting added to games, it became a much more prevalent force in conveying information to the player.

With that line of thinking, it would be advantageous for a level designer to guide a player without actually leading him by the hand. If players feel that a game is telling them where to go and explicitly guiding their actions, they will feel as if the choices they make are insignificant.

Games such as *Bioshock* use this to great effect, utilizing the environment in such a way to show players examples of what they will be experiencing later in the game through the use of posters as well as creative usage of lighting to guide players to locations as well as clever mesh placements.

A level designer can supplement the pacing, ecology, and environment of a level by applying aspects from psychology and architecture. Successful implementation of these concepts results in an immersive experience for the player, who is oblivious to the efforts taken by the designer to guide them along the way.

Now, I could write a whole book on creating levels for different types of game, but in this project, I will briefly share the things I wish I knew before I started working on levels in the game industry.

Mission Briefing

In this project, we will focus on building environments by creating a small, fairly polished map. We will be using the map that we create in this project on the next mission, where we create a fully functional inventory system!

Why Is It Awesome?

After this project you will have a firm grounding in how to design environments that feel realistic as well as how to use assets in the most effective way possible. You will also acquire a lot of information that will be useful in building much larger environments.

Your Hotshot Objectives

As usual, we will be following a simple step-by-step process from the beginning to the end to complete the project. Here is an outline of our tasks:

- ▶ Building the stage
- ▶ Creating the backdrop
- ▶ Placing assets into the level

Mission Checklist

This particular mission has no requirements to get started aside from knowing how to use the **Translate**, **Rotation**, and **Scaling** widgets, so feel free to jump in!

Should you need a bit of a refresher, Unreal provides documentation about the widgets at `http://udn.epicgames.com/Three/UnrealEdUserGuide.html#Interactive Transformation`.

By default, UDK uses a 2x2 split-viewport configuration. One thing to note for newcomers is that the viewport configuration I use is a 1x2 split, so images may be a bit off from the traditional. Should you wish to follow along exactly, you can set your viewport to be the same by going to **View | Viewport Configuration | 1x2 Split**.

Building the stage

Once we start up UDK, let's try to get an environment up with the minimal work possible. To do this, we will use the default map as a base and then adapt it to fit our workflow. With that said, let's get to creating!

Prepare for Lift Off

Before we start working on the project, we must first create a new map. To do this we must first go to **File | New Level...** and from the pop up that appears, select one of the top four options (**Afternoon Lighting** was chosen for the images you'll see here, but it doesn't matter which you choose).

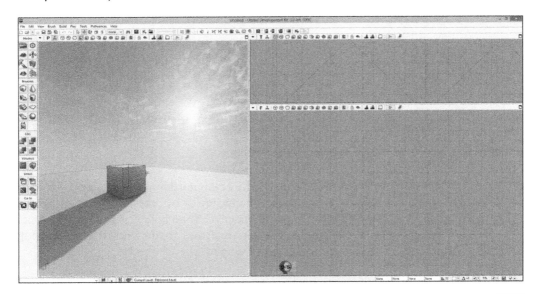

Engage Thrusters

Now that we have a base level to work in, let's start building our game!

1. With the level created, bring up the **World Properties** menu by going to **View | World Properties** from the menu bar at the top of the UDK interface. Type Game Type in the search bar at the top of the **World Properties** menu, which will bring up the **Game Type** menu and the options relevant to us. From there, change the drop-down menus for both **Default Game Type** and **Game Type For PIE** to **UDKGame**. While we are there, in the **Zone Info** section under **Kill Z**, set the value to -1000.

2. Back in the Perspective viewport, delete the box in the center of the level and the ground by clicking on them and pressing the *Delete* key.

3. Enter **Geometry Mode** by clicking on the three-dimensional cube located on the **Modes** section of the toolbar on the left-hand side or by pressing *Shift + 2*. Click on the builder brush within the front perspective. Then hold *Ctrl* and *Alt* and click slightly above and to the left of the builder brush and create a box that selects both the vertices that you can see from that viewpoint.

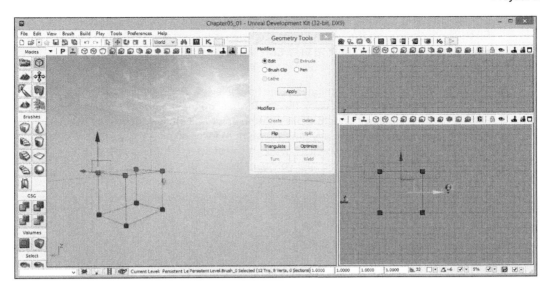

4. When you release the mouse, you will notice that all four points on the square have been selected. Right-click on the upper-right-hand-side point to move the translation tool to your position. Confirm that your **Toggle Drag Grid** option is enabled (located in the bottom-right corner next to the **DrawScale** options) and also that the number shown to the left-hand side of it is **32**. Drag the top of the brush down to 32 units above the bottom of the box.

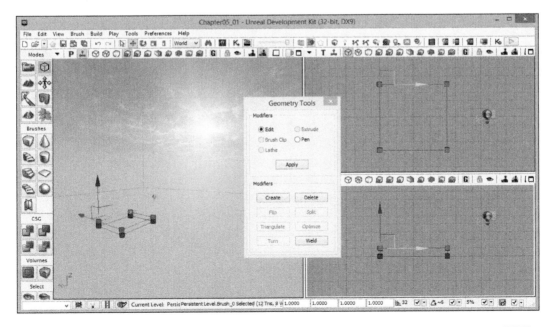

5. Change the grid spacing to **128** by pressing the *]* key two times. Extend the floor to fill the spaces around the yellow lines (Lightmass Importance Volume) by selecting each of the edges from the Top viewport and dragging them out.

 Just as a friendly reminder, while having a viewport selected you can zoom in/out from it using the scroll wheel on the mouse. Dragging while holding the right mouse button down will move your view of the viewport. Also, if at any time you want to focus on an actor, you can press the *Home* key while having an object selected. This is also very useful to *teleport* to a spot you want to work on.

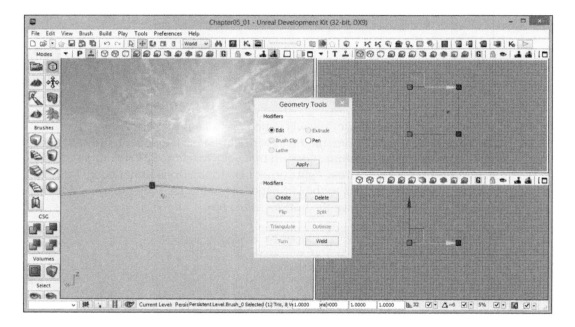

6. Next, open the **Content Browser** window by going to **View | Browser Windows | Content Browser** and type `Cobble` into the search bar at the top. Click on `Material'Castle_Assets.Textures.M_Cobble_02'` to select it.

7. With that selected, click on **Add Brush** to create our floor.

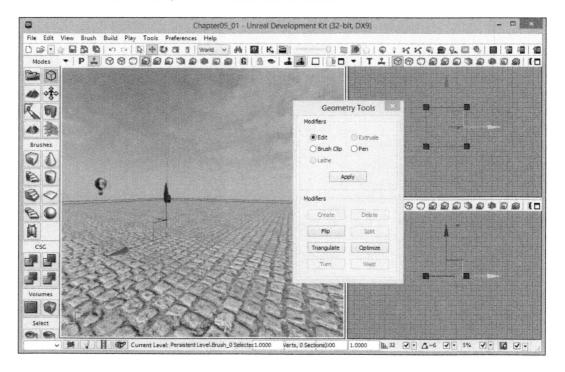

After placing a single brush in our level, we don't really need the builder brush again. Unless you are creating something other than a box, you can just duplicate brushes and mold them using the geometry tool to quickly shape out areas, which usually makes them much quicker to build.

If you too feel that you can live without the builder brush, you may press the *B* key to toggle the building brush off (this key can be used to toggle the building brush on and off).

8. Now that we have a floor, let's place some static meshes. Go into the **Content Browser** window and select `StaticMesh'Castle_Assets.Meshes.SM_House_01'`.

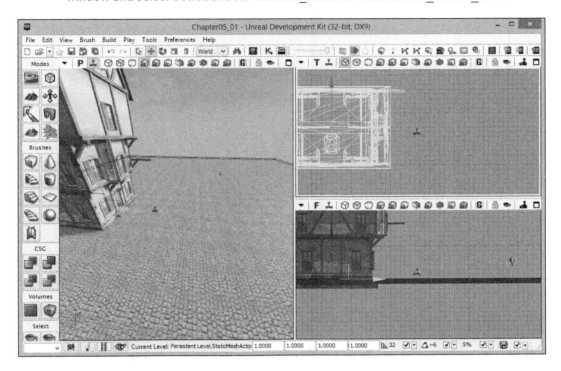

9. After placing the first house, hold the *Alt* key and drag to create two other houses surrounding the player from three sides. Rotate these two houses so that the sides that the player would see are different from one other.

Humans are very good at detecting patterns, and repetition is one of them. I'm sure if you took a look at the following screenshot, you will see the bottom texture repeating; however, at eye level it is a lot more difficult to tell. Repetition is also easily visible when using the same model twice, facing the same way. By having them face different directions, we start the process of making them unique.

After we place the houses, take some time to make the houses appear different from each other. One of the nice things this model does is to separate the UVs of the house to different materials.

UV mapping is the process of using a two-dimensional image to provide color data to essentially *paint* a three-dimensional model. U and V are the axes of that texture; we don't use x, y, or z as those refer to its position in three-dimensional space. If you have used the Surface Properties feature in UDK before, you are effectively modifying the UV mapping of the CSG (which we will be doing in the next section). Artists are very creative with UVs and we can actually use the same model with different UVs to produce different-looking objects, which is what we'll be doing next!

We can use this to make every house unique even though we're using the same model.

10. Select one of the houses by clicking on it and then pressing *F4* to access its Properties menu. From the search bar at the top, type in `Material` to see the material's property under the static mesh actor. Press the **+** button four times.

 If you'd like to see what exactly it is we're changing, you can go into the Static Mesh Editor by double-clicking on the house's mesh in the **Content Browser** window, typing `Material` in the search bar, and then clicking on each of the slots. Whatever is highlighted is the overloading the material will change.

11. Go to the **Content Browser** window and type in `WoodBoards` into the search bar. You can select either of the two options, but I selected `Material'E3_Demo.Textures.M_WoodBoards_03'` for the **[0]** place.

12. After that, type in the word `Plaster` and choose one for the **[1]** place. I used `Material'E3_Demo.Textures.M_Plaster_03'`.

13. From there, type in `building` and select one of the three houses shown. I chose `Material'E3_Demo.Textures.M_Building_02'` for the **[2]** place.

14. Finally, in the **[3]** place, search for `roof` and pick a rooftop for your building. I personally picked `Material'E3_Demo.Textures.M_Rooftile_02'`. This has created a house that uses the same model as the other two and looks quite different from the other two houses.

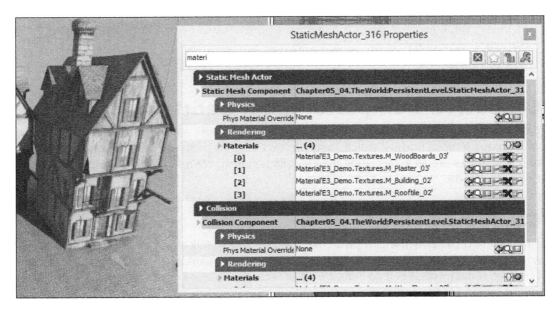

15. Take the other house and change it in the same way, keeping in mind what materials to use in each slot. From now on in this mission, any time we place another house we'll take some time to change it slightly from the others. To give you a view of what they look like without lighting, I turned the viewport to **Unlit** as shown in the following screenshot:

Objective Complete - Mini Debriefing

We now have the base through which we will have the player walk through within our level, with unique-looking houses, which, when inside the game, will lessen the player's realization that the houses are all in fact using the exact same mesh. We also covered a quick view of Geometry Mode.

Classified Intel

This project is basically the only place that I will be able to talk about level design. I could write an entire book just about this subject, and as you're working in Unreal, I may assume you have some interest in it so here is a bit of recap on building environments.

Creating environments and the basics of level design

Before we delve into utilizing the interface described previously and also putting to use the knowledge gained so far, let us delve into some theory.

CSG brushes

We've been throwing the word brushes and CSG around a lot, so it's a good idea to define what that actually is. **Constructive Solid Geometry (CSG)** is a term used in UDK for world geometry, which UDK creates from the brushes you create in the level. **Brushes** on the other hand are three-dimensional objects that are used to define space. We define that space in four different ways: Add, Subtract, Intersect, and Deintersect.

Static meshes

Static meshes on the other hand are polygonal creations that can also be used for the formation of a game level in Unreal/UDK that are not moving within the world. These are often brought into UDK from a three-dimensional modeling package, giving us limitless possibilities for what to make in terms of world creation, given some basic three-dimensional asset-creation skills from the developer.

The differences between CSG brushes and static meshes

So, what are the differences between using brushes and static meshes? Why use one or the other?

You should be aware that today static meshes are really the professional's choice for world creation in UDK, for two simple reasons: performance and aesthetics. It is much faster to use static meshes (provided you use quality ones!) and they will look much, much better than brushes. Brushes have also had or led to their fair share of problems, such as causing holes, and static meshes have provided the much-needed solution in resolving such inefficiencies.

However, there is still a place for brushes. In the game industry, many game designers will block out a level using brushes and get the scripting working correctly. This way, the designer is able to focus on making the game fun and ensuring that the functionality of the level is completed (to ensure that everything will work). When the level is completed, the designers will give the level to an environmental artist who will then replace the brushes with meshes that they've created aside from a few things such as maybe the floor and some walls. That said, all studios are different, so a workflow in one company could be completely different from another's.

A quick refresher on the different kinds of CSG operations:

- **Add**: This uses the last selection of the brush-builder mode, and with that as a template creates an additive brush in the level
- **Subtract**: This is the same as the previous one, but in this there is the creation of a subtractive brush
- **Intersect**: This will only show the section of a brush that overlaps other intersecting brushes, with the rest not being visible
- **Deintersect**: This results in the inverse of the previous operation

 I personally use the add operation for 90 percent of the brushes I use, as I like consistency, but subtract can be nice for things like doorways, and the others can be used for neat effects. Just be sure that you stick to the grid and do not create holes in the geometry!

In this section, we began to explore Geometry Mode and how it can be used by us. For those building levels outside of this project, I feel it is important to talk about how we can use Geometry Mode to create gameplay areas quickly and effectively when you're working on levels of your own.

Setting up the workflow

You may have noticed a grid of sorts in all the viewports other than the Perspective one. We will be using the grid as a guideline in the creation of our levels in much the same way that you would use paper to draw things out, which is something some level designers I know do to get the general feel of an area. Starting to build a general area needs to have planning ahead of time to have a basic idea of how you want to place buildings as well as an idea of how you want to guide the traversal of the player.

As previously mentioned, pressing the [and] keys in the editor will decrease and increase the grid snap points respectively, making the level more or less detailed in your brush placement. For the purposes of this book, unless I say differently, I have my grid spacing set to 32. Some people will want to use a smaller area, but I argue that when blocking something out we really only care about the big picture and getting the overall feel of the area. In case your brush is not aligned to the grid, you can right-click on the vertices and it will automatically snap it onto the grid.

Working with the grid is a fundamental way of making sure that you are not getting any holes and/or overlays of your brushes when creating a level. This is another way to make sure that your subtractive brushes will work as you intend them to; however, I never use subtractive brushes if I can at all help it.

One thing to note when using Geometry Mode is that you will not see any changes that we make when editing in Geometry Mode until we *build* our CSG brushes again.

Some keyboard tips

Holding *Ctrl* and *Alt* at the same time and dragging will allow you to select all objects that are contained within it. This is known as marquee selection. If you are in Geometry Mode, opening it will allow you to select individual/overlapping vertices and will allow you to increase or decrease the size of your brushes very easily. We will be using this to create our buildings in the next section.

Another useful tip is that if you hold *Ctrl* and drag the left mouse button anywhere in a viewport, it will move the brush, actor, and/or vertices that you have selected from any position. This is a good way to move objects without having to rely on the Transform widget.

If you just click on a brush in the Perspective viewport, it will select the face of the object. While this is nice for putting a material on the brush, on the other viewports it will select the brush for editing. If you hold *Ctrl* and *Shift* and click on your map, you will notice that the brush that you clicked on is selected. However, it may sometimes not pick the brush that you think you're selecting, which is why I primarily use the Top and/or Side viewport.

Creating the backdrop

Now that we have the area our player will be able to walk through, let's restrict access to that area and minimize the chance of the player realizing it is there.

Prepare for Lift Off

In order to restrict access to areas, we need to have walls that the player cannot jump over. Now, it would be possible to just create BlockingVolumes, but just having the players stop walking into an area breaks immersion immediately. Having logical reasons as to why a player cannot enter an area is much easier to believe; walls or gates tend to be good ways to do that.

Engage Thrusters

So, with that said, let's build some walls.

1. Now that we have the basis for our area, we need to enclose the gameplay space. For that, we will need to build walls. Enter into **Geometry Mode** and hold down *Ctrl* and *Shift*; then click on the floor that we have created from steps 3 to 7 in the previous task, in order to select it.

2. In the Front viewport, go to the **Wireframe** mode (*Alt + 2*) and then hold *Alt* and drag the floor 32 units above the floor to create a copy. Hold the *Ctrl* and *Alt* keys, grab the two vertices on the right-hand side of the Top viewport, and drag the new brush to the left to match against the house that we created previously.

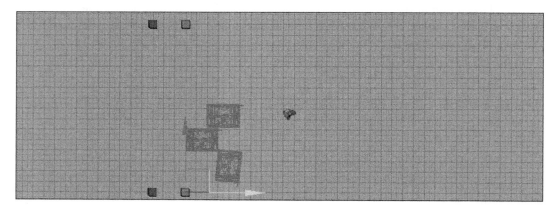

3. After that, select the top of the cube and bring it up to the edge of the second story of the houses.

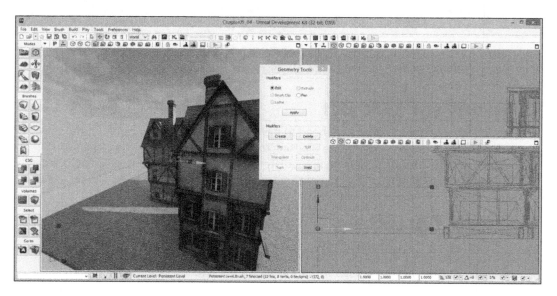

It's worth noting again that you will not see changes made in Geometry Mode until you build your map.

4. Duplicate this wall to create four walls that contain the three houses with a little wiggle room on the right-hand side.

5. Build your map by going to **Build | Build All**.

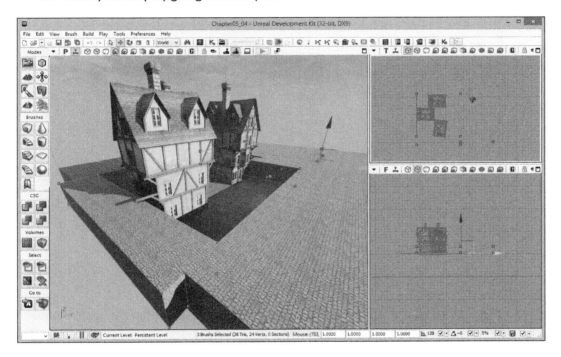

6. Click on one of our newly created wall surfaces inside the Perspective viewport. Right-click on it and go to **Select Surfaces | Adjacent Walls** to select all of the walls surrounding our houses. Open up the **Content Browser** window and select the texture to use for your walls; I personally used `Material'Castle_Assets. Textures.M_CobbleStone'`. Finally, right-click once again on the wall and select **Apply Material : M_CobbleStone**.

7. With that done, press *F5* to access the **Surface Properties** menu. In the **Scaling** section, change the **Simple** value to 3.0 and then click on **Apply**.

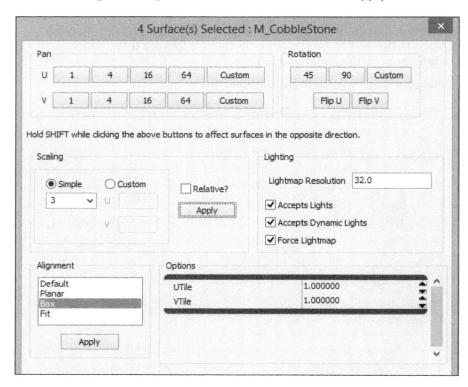

8. Adjust the UVs of the brush by clicking on the buttons under the **Pan** section until you are satisfied with where the stones are.

When working with materials on CSG brushes, useful shortcuts include the use of *Alt* and right-clicking on a brush surface, which allows you to grab a material (the same as selecting it in the **Content Browser** window), and holding down *Alt* and left-clicking, which allows you to quickly place your selected material in the world.

9. Now that we have some walls, let's create some background material to make our world look more realistic. Open up the **Content Browser** window and select the mesh `StaticMesh'Castle_Assets.Meshes.SM_Walls_Front_01'`. Now, with the mesh selected, right-click anywhere on the Perspective viewport and select **New Static Mesh : Castle_Assets.Meshes.SM_Walls_Front_01**. You will notice that, unlike the usual behavior, the mesh is off in the distance somewhere. Use the translate tool to move it so that it is slightly below the walls we just finished creating.

10. You may notice that this mesh has a doorway at the end of it. With that in mind, let's create a ring of these walled towers around our environment. Create a duplicate of this mesh by holding *Alt* and dragging it away. Once you create a copy, translate and rotate it in such a way that the doorway from the first mesh goes into the new mesh's tower.

11. We will keep on placing towers to fill in visible doorways, continuing to create a ring around our game's environment. When you are finished, you should have something like that shown in the following screenshot:

This provides us with a world outside of our level that players can see but can't actually access. This covers up the skybox at eye level, making sure that players cannot see that the game world goes on forever, and actually helps with the suspension of disbelief needed to believe they are in a real place. Take a look at most first-person games and you'll notice how level designers have cleverly created environments that seem much larger than they actually are.

12. Next, duplicate the houses we created earlier and place them on the second story in the area from the wall to the castle walls. Rotate them in such a way that all of them aren't facing the same way, helping to reduce a repetitive pattern.

Objective Complete - Mini Debriefing

At this point, our level has a backdrop that we can believe is a medieval town of some sort. This backdrop blocks our access to the skybox, giving us details of our world allowing players to believe their environment is a lot larger than they really have access to. Now that we are finished with developing a flow to our level, let's take some time to place meshes and polish the level up!

Placing assets in the level

The final 20 percent of the work required to finish a level tends to feel like 80 percent of it. Creating an environment that looks believable is done in small pieces. Tiny imperfections make the world look like it has a human touch. In this section, we add little features to make the level look that much more like a fully fleshed-out world.

Engage Thrusters

Now that we have a basic environment, let's place some little touches to make the place look at least somewhat lived in.

1. Go into the **Content Browser** window and select `StaticMesh'Castle_Assets.Meshes.SM_VendorCrate_01_E'`. Next to **PlayerStart**, place a crate in order to block access to other areas of the map, by right-clicking and selecting **Add Static Mesh : Castle_Assets.Meshes.SM_VendorCrate_01_E**.

2. Duplicate the box to create a stack of them that look as if they were naturally placed. This can be done by rotating objects slightly as well as changing the scale on objects in the upper crates and making them half the size of the larger ones (by opening the object's Properties window and changing the **DrawScale** value to `0.5`), using the same mesh to create a variety of objects.

Working on the grid is the level designer's best friend, especially while prototyping and creating an environment. The truth is that the real world is quite messy and, as stated previously, it can be quite easy to see repeated objects unless you take steps to prevent that.

Doing things in order to break symmetry, such as facing objects in different directions and breaking the repetitiveness, can go a long way in making your environment more believable.

If you place an object above another or on the floor, you can press the *End* key in order to have it automatically drop until it *hits* the floor. This can be quite useful to make sure things are fitting exactly and that there isn't any extra space between the object and the floor.

3. Do the same on the other side, making sure to block the entire way there. Then place a crate between each of the middle houses so players will see objects when they look there. Finally, create a PointLight (hold down *L* and click in the Perspective viewport) with a **Brightness** value of 0.6 in the center of the three houses on the first level.

 At this point, you may realize that I am trying to lead the player to move to the middle of the three houses, as that's where I will have the player collect items for the inventory that we will be creating in the next mission.

4. At this point, to add even more variety, I added a cart (StaticMesh'E3_Demo. Meshes.SM_Cart_01') to the side of the boxes. Finally, in the section between of the two houses, I placed two vendor stalls (StaticMesh'Castle_Assets. Meshes.SM_VendorStand_01_A' and StaticMesh'Castle_Assets.Meshes. SM_VendorStand_04_G'), with some food (StaticMesh'Castle_Assets. Meshes.SM_VendorGoods_05_A').

5. Build your map by going to **Build | Build All**. Once you finish, you should have something that looks like the following screenshot:

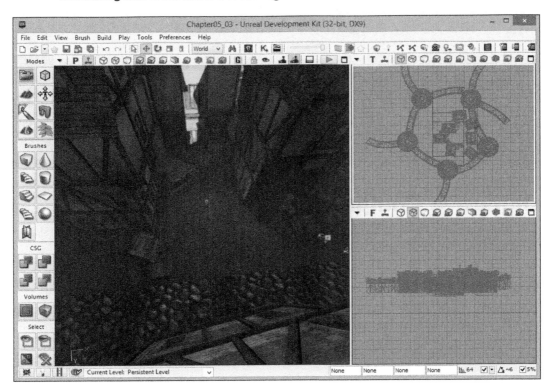

There is much more that you can do to add additional detail to your environments. Epic's very own Epic Citadel map shows just how simple it can be to use modular pieces to make varied environments while also doing it so effectively that it can run on a phone and on a web browser. The map is available for you to look at and examine at your leisure in the `UDKGame\Content\Maps\Mobile` folder of your UDK installation.

6. Save your project (**File | Save All**) and start your game by pressing *F8* or going to **Play | In Editor** on the main toolbar.

Objective Complete - Mini Debriefing

And with that, we have a fully fleshed-out area that would not look out of place within a fantasy RPG, which will be perfect to use in our next mission!

Classified Intel

In this section, we briefly touched on using light as well as object duplication. Let's take some time to talk just a little bit about how important these factors actually are.

I see the light

Spending time to make your lighting look as good as possible is well worth it; there are people in the industry whose entire job is positioning lighting in the best way possible.

An environment's lighting can be used in many different ways to affect what a player can do. Primarily, light draws focus to things, and as humans are creatures that like the light they tend to travel towards it. Darkness and the unknown are uncomfortable areas for players to be in; and not lighting some areas as much as others adds to the foreboding nature that those areas could take.

Monolith's *F.E.A.R.* series of games does this quite nicely by turning an office into an intense and dangerous place to be in, even though you are fully armed and equipped to handle anything that may come your way.

Seeing double – duplication

Duplicating things that we have already created, such as walls or buildings, is an effective way of blocking out an environment very quickly. What we care about most here is creating the best gameplay possible, so we pay less attention to the fine details and basically want to just block out an area so we can iterate as quickly as possible. After all, you're a lot more willing to get rid of a huge box than a ridiculously detailed office building.

With the brushes created, we can give the level to your team's environmental artist (or to you if you are gifted with three-dimensional modeling knowledge), who will change the CSG brushes into meshes to place in our level to give it the visual flair that we are looking for.

Mission Accomplished

Again, we've only touched the tip of the iceberg, but we got our feet just a little deeper in the large pool that is environment creation. We have created an environment that looks quite varied using only a small amount of objects and resources, showing just how far we can push a small number of assets.

With what we covered, however, you should have a much better foundation for creating new levels of your own. Let's take one final look at what we have accomplished:

You Ready to go Gung HO? A Hotshot Challenge

Through this project we have learned how to create an environment within a short period of time, but there is still plenty of things we can do! How about you take some time between projects and try to complete the following:

- ▸ Take time to add additional meshes into our level, such as barrels and buckets.

- ▸ Extend the gameplay area of the level with an additional path to get to three building centers. Experiment with how to lead the player to that area taking into account the mesh placement and lighting.

- ▸ For those experienced with modeling, spend some time learning about how to create modular environments, which is a way to create professional-looking levels really quickly with minimal assets, to have a large variety of functionality. For starters, read Kevin Johnstone's slides for his talk named *Modular Environment Design: Or how I learned to stop worrying and love the grid* at `http://www.kevinjohnstone.com/Help/Modular%20Environment%20Design.rar`.

- ▸ After that, check out Thiago Klafke's excellent tutorial on how to build modular environments, at `http://www.thiagoklafke.com/modularenvironments.html`.

Project 6

Dynamic Loot

As a real-time interactive simulation, video games provide players with an experience where their actions directly affect what happens within the game's world. This can be done in many different ways, such as having an avatar that traverses the game environment. For games wanting to do more, you can also provide ways to interact with the world, such as fighting and defeating opponents. However, changing the actual objects within the game space gives the player a much better sense of agency in the world.

Games such as *The Sims* allow players to place items around their house using a grid. Other games such as Bethesda's *The Elder Scrolls: Skyrim* allow players to pick up, buy, sell, or drop any item within the game's world.

In this project, we will be creating a dynamic object that the player may alter at runtime in order to pick them up, drop them elsewhere making use of rigid-body physics, or toggle the player's ability to hold it in his hand as he traverses the game environment.

Mission Briefing

We will provide functionality similar to *The Elder Scrolls: Skyrim* in allowing our players to pick up objects within the game world. The players will also be able to drop them wherever they would like and carry them about. All of this functionality will be done through Kismet before moving them to a custom inventory system, which is explained in the next project. The following screenshot shows a dynamic object that we will create in a game with all of the expected functionality:

Why Is It Awesome?

After this project, we will have an object with which players can interact in ways that are not provided by default in UDK, but that have become standard in Western RPGs.

Your Hotshot Objectives

As usual, we will be following a simple step-by-step process from the beginning to the end to complete the project. Here is an outline of our tasks:

- ▶ Creating a dynamic object
- ▶ Picking up the object
- ▶ Dropping the object
- ▶ Equipping the object

Mission Checklist

This mission assumes that you have completed the previous two projects or at least are comfortable with what was done in them as this project is built on that knowledge and the content created in those projects.

Creating a dynamic object

We now have an environment in which we can interact. With this basis, we can lay down the framework to develop our customized inventory. To get started, let's get our item into the game's world and prepare Kismet to pick up and drop the object.

Prepare for Lift Off

Before we start working on the project, we need to open up the map that we created in the previous project. If you are just starting to join us, you can find this in the Chapter 5 folder (UDKHotshot_Chapter5.udk) of the sample code that can be downloaded from the support page on Packt Publishing's website, at www.packtpub.com/support.

Engage Thrusters

Now that we have our base level to work in, let's get an object created!

1. Open up the **Content Browser** window by going into **View | Browser Windows | Content Browser**. Inside the **Content Browser** window, find the object that you wish to pick up and carry. I'll be creating a torch that I can carry around to make the area more visually interesting. Select `StaticMesh'GenericFoliage01.Ruins.Mesh. SM_UDK_Torch01'` by clicking on it.

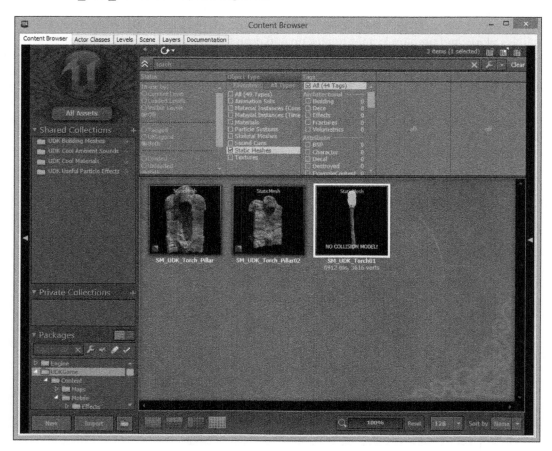

2. Create a copy of the torch by right-clicking and selecting **Create a Copy...**. Change the **Package** value to Hotshot06, clear out the **Grouping** field, and set the **New Name** value to CarryingTorch. After that, click on the **OK** button. Save the package that you just created by right-clicking on it and selecting **Save**.

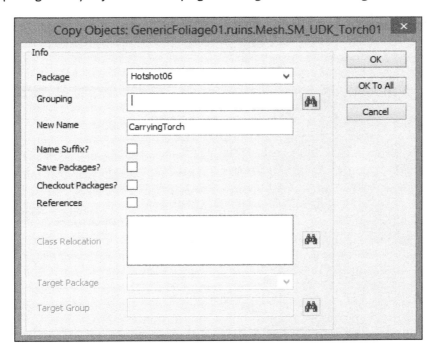

3. Double-click on the new mesh to open up the Static Mesh Editor. Inside the editor, click on the **Collision | Auto Convex Collision** option from the top menu. Leaving the default options is fine; just click on the **Apply** button on the window that pops up. Check the **Can Become Dynamic** option. Uncheck the **Use Simple Box Collision** and **Use Simple Line Collision** options.

Meshes that do not have a Simplified Collision defined cannot be transformed into KActors. If the mesh does not move when you shoot it, the first thing to check is that it has Simplified Collision.

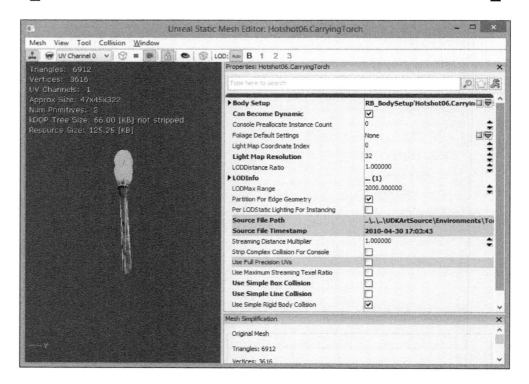

4. Now, go into the middle of our level with the newly created torch selected in the **Content Browser** window. We want this object to be dynamic and react to the environment when the player drops it, so we want it to be a **KActor** (the K stands for kinetic, relating to motion). Right-click on the ground and select **Add UT Rigid Body : Hotshot06.CarryingTorch**.

 You can also drag-and-drop an object into UDK and place them where you want. However, in this case you will need to convert the created object to a rigid body.

5. You'll notice that the torch is quite large; let's fix that. Click on the torch and press *F4* to access its Properties window, and change the **Scale** value to 0.25. Inside of the **KActor** section, find the **Wake on Level Start** property and check it. If you were to start the game now, you will notice it fall onto the ground. Success!

6. Now let's do a few more things to spice this torch up. Find
   `ParticleSystem'GenericFoliage01.ruins.FX.P_UDK_TorchFire01'` in
   the **Content Browser** window. Add it into our level and place it on top of the first
   part of the torch that we've created. Access the emitter's properties by pressing *F4*.
   Click on the lock icon to lock your selection and type into the search bar `base`. Click
   on the torch and then click on the green arrow to attach the particle system to the
   torch. Now if the torch ever moves, the fire attached to it also will.

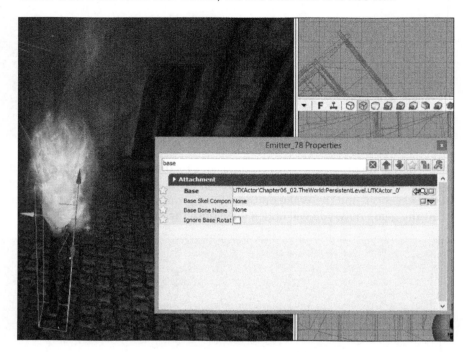

7. Now, what would the point in a torch be if it didn't emit light? Let's create a light that will follow the torch anywhere we put it in the world. Access the **Actor Classes** window by selecting **View | Browser Windows | Actor Classes**. Inside the window that pops up, type `light` into the **Search** box. From there, click on the **PointLightMoveable** option.

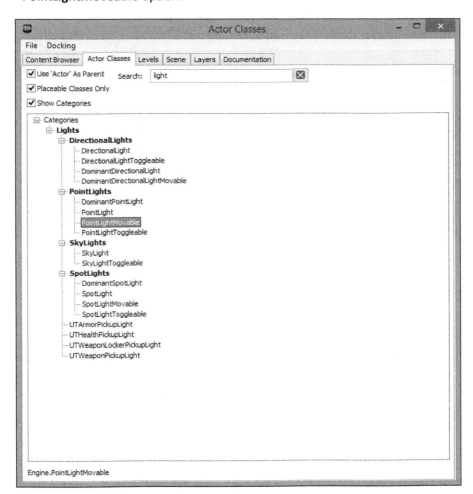

8. Right-click on the top part of the torch in the Perspective viewport and select **Add PointLightMoveable Here**. Use the translate tool to adjust the light until it is inside the torch. Open up the light's Properties window using *F4*. Change the **Brightness** value to 2.0, the **Light Color** value to an orange fire-like color, and the **Base** value to the torch, in the same way we did previously. To make it easier to see the effect the light has in the world, change the **Radius** value to 256.

9. Build everything including our lighting by selecting **Build | Build All**. Once that is finished, save your project (**File | Save All**) and start your game by pressing *F8* or selecting **Play | In Editor** on the main toolbar.

Objective Complete - Mini Debriefing

Now we have a nice little object that can be useful for us to use in our game world that interacts with the environment in a believable manner.

Picking up an object

We have our lovely object created; now add in just a few more components and then use Kismet to make our object appear to be picked up.

Engage Thrusters

With that in mind, let's use Kismet to make our object appear to be picked up.

1. Now, move your Perspective viewport to an area that the player cannot see. When we pick up an object, this is the area where the object will go until we drop it. To put it here, we need a PathNode to show where the object will be teleported. Right-click on the ground and select **Add Actor | Add PathNode**.

2. Now, we need an indicator to know where to drop the object in our inventory. To drop it directly in front of where the player is spawned, we need to create a **PathNode_Dynamic** PathNode. To do this, move your camera from the Top viewport to where your player spawn point is. Access the **Actor Classes** window by selecting **View | Browser Windows | Actor Classes**. In the window that pops up, type `pathnode` into the **Search** box. From there, click on the **PathNode_Dynamic** option.

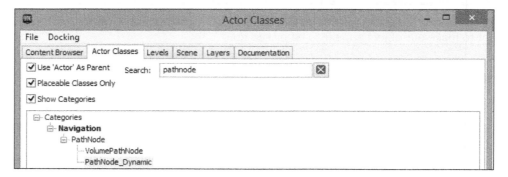

3. In the Perspective viewport move the camera to the player's spawn point, and in front of the arrow pointing out of the spawn point right-click and select **Add PathNode_Dynamic Here**. Rotate the object to face the same rotation as the one where the player is spawned and translate it to some place in front of the player. This will be acting as an area where the player will drop our object into the world, so I would suggest around eye level. Once you are finished with the placement, build the AI Paths by selecting **Build | AI Paths**.

Just a quick reminder that this is not the general use of PathNodes; they are primarily used for **bot navigation**. You may notice that your AI Path line may be of a different color than the green one that I have shown. The coloration of the path line tells you what kind of a path it is and how wide it is, so if you're wondering why it is a certain color, here is a little guide to help you out:

- ▶ Blue – Narrow path
- ▶ Green – Normal width
- ▶ White – Wide path
- ▶ Pink – Very wide path
- ▶ Orange – Flying path, narrow
- ▶ Light Orange – Flying path, wide
- ▶ Light Purple – requires high jump (higher than normal jump capability)
- ▶ Yellow – Forced path
- ▶ Purple – Advanced path

4. Finally, create a **Trigger_Dynamic** trigger by opening up the **Actor Classes** window by selecting **View | Browser Windows | Actor Classes**. In the window that pops up, type `trigger` into the **Search** box. From there, click on the **Trigger_Dynamic** option.

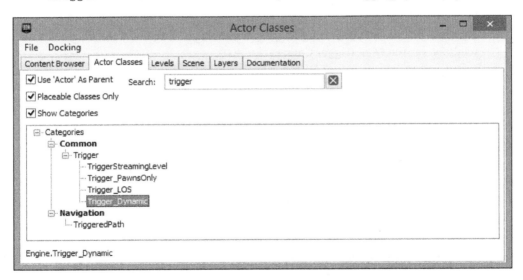

5. Go to the torch we created in the previous section and place the **Trigger_Dynamic** trigger on it by right-clicking and selecting **Add Trigger_Dynamic Here**. Then translate the trigger to fit the torch, and go into the Properties window to set the **Base** property as the torch so that trigger will follow the torch.

6. We've now finished the setup. Now we need to create our Kismet for interactions. To do this we need to enter Kismet. Make sure that the trigger is selected by clicking on it and then open up Kismet by clicking on the **K** icon located on the top toolbar.

7. Inside the main sequence, create a **Trigger_Dynamic_1 Used** event by right-clicking and selecting **New Event Using Trigger_Dynamic_1 | Used**. In the event's Properties window, set the **Max Trigger Count** value to 0.

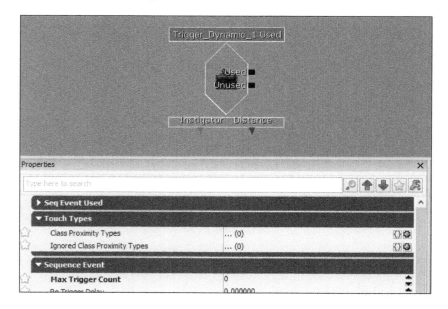

8. To the right-hand side of the **Trigger_Dynamic_1 Used** event, create a **Teleport**
    action by selecting **New Action | Actor | Teleport**. Under the **Target** section go into
    the Perspective viewport and use the torch **KActor**. Then go to the PathNode that
    is outside the player's sight and use it in the **Destination** section. Connect the **Used**
    output from the **Trigger_Dynamic_1 Used** action to the **In** input of the **Teleport** action.

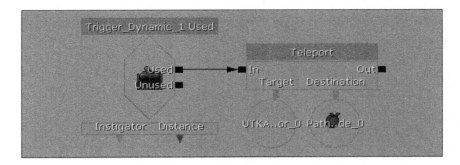

9. To the right-hand side of the **Teleport** action, create a **Play Sound** action by
    right-clicking and selecting **New Action | Sound | Play Sound**. Pick a Sound Cue
    that you like to put in the **Play Sound** property; I used `SoundCue'A_Character_`
    `Footsteps.FootSteps.A_Character_Footstep_GlassBrokenJumpCue'`.

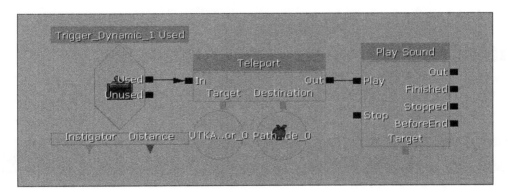

10. Save your project (**File | Save All**) and start your game by pressing *F8* or selecting **Play | In Editor** on the main toolbar.

Objective Complete - Mini Debriefing

Now if you use (press the *E* key by default) the torch, it will disappear into our inventory. Of course, we will be doing more things on the Scaleform side of things to actually store objects we collect.

Dropping the object

All right, we have now seen that it is simple enough to pick up an object. But what if we want to bring it back into the world?

Engage Thrusters

Simple enough. Let's do that now.

1. Open up Kismet once again. Create a **Player Spawned** event by right-clicking and selecting **New Event | Player | Player Spawned**.

2. To the right-hand side of the **Player Spawned** event, create an **Attach to Actor**
   action by right-clicking and selecting **New Action | Actor | Attach to Actor**. Under
   Target, create a **Player** variable by right-clicking and selecting **New Variable | Player
   | Player**, and by unchecking the **All Players** option in the Properties window. Go
   into the Perspective viewport and find the **PathNode_Dynamic** option that we put
   in front of the player's spawn point and click on it. Under **Attachment**, right-click
   and select **New Object Var using PathNode_Dynamic_0**. Click on the **PathNode_
   Dynamic** variable and under the **Var Name** option put in DropPoint as we'll be
   referring to it by its name later in the project. Click on the **Attach to Actor** action to
   access its Properties window. Check the **Use Relative Offset** option and change the
   X value to 200.

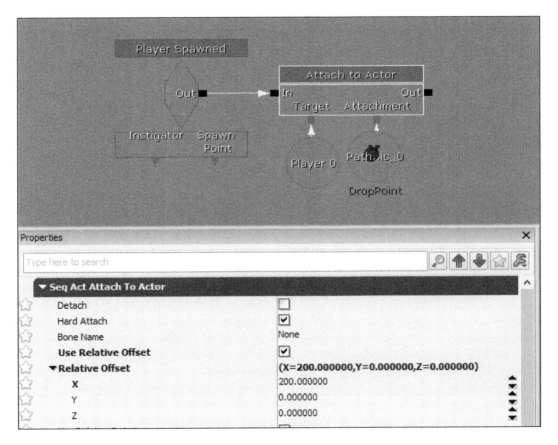

3. To the right-hand side of the **Attach to Actor** action, leaving some space, we need to create a **Key/Button Pressed** event by right-clicking and selecting **New Event | Input | Key/Button Pressed**. Click on the event to access the Properties window and press the **+** button under the **Input Names** section and place R in **[0]**. Finally, uncheck the **Enabled** option inside the **Sequence Event** section.

4. To the right-hand side of the **Key/Button Pressed** event, create a **Trace** action by right-clicking and selecting **New Action | Misc | Trace**. Under **Start** create a **Player** variable. At the **End** section create a named variable (by right-clicking and selecting **New Variable | Named Variable**) with a **Var Name** value of DropPoint. Connect **Pressed** from the **Key/Button Pressed** event to the **In** input of the **Trace** action.

5. To the right-hand side and below the **Trace** action, create a **Play Sound** action by right-clicking and selecting **New Action | Sound | Play Sound**. This Sound Cue will be used to tell the player that he cannot drop the item because something is on in the way. For the **Play Sound** property, I used SoundCue'a_interface.menu. UT3MenuErrorCue'. Connect the **Obstructed** output from the **Trace** action to the **Play** input of the **Play Sound** action.

6. Next, to the right-hand side of the **Trace** action we will create a **Teleport** action by selecting **New Action | Actor | Teleport**. Under the **Target** section go into the Perspective viewport and use the torch **KActor** that we used previously. Create a named variable (by right-clicking and selecting **New Variable | Named Variable**) with a **Var Name** value of DropPoint to set as the destination.

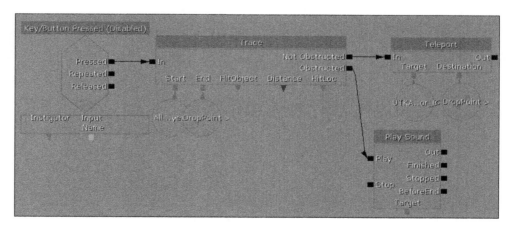

7. To the right-hand side of the **Teleport** action create a **Play Sound** action by right-clicking and selecting **New Action | Sound | Play Sound**. This Sound Cue will be used to tell the player that he dropped the item. For the **Play Sound** property, I used SoundCue'A_Character_Footsteps.FootSteps.A_Character_Footstep_ GlassBrokenLandCue'. Connect the **Out** output from the **Teleport** action to the **Play** input of the **Play Sound** action.

8. Then, create a **Toggle** action by right-clicking and selecting **New Action | Toggle | Toggle**. Click on the **Event** section and drag and release on the **Key/Button Pressed** event. Connect the **Out** output from the **Play Sound** action to the **Turn Off** input of the **Toggle** action.

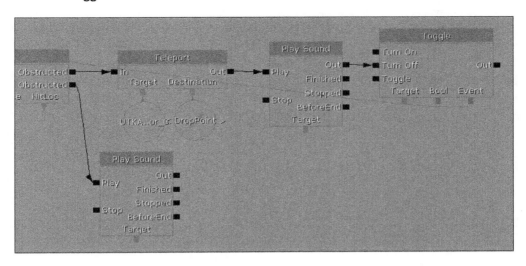

9. Finally, create another **Toggle** action to the right-hand side of the **Play Sound** action that we created earlier. Connect the **Event** section to the **Key/Button Pressed** event, and then the **Out** output of the **Play Sound** action to the **Turn On** input of this second **Toggle** action.

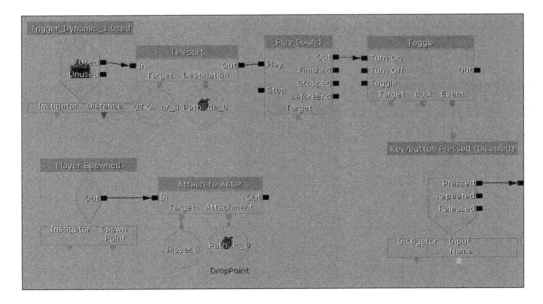

10. Save your project (**File** | **Save All**) and start your game by pressing *F8* or selecting **Play** | **In Editor** on the main toolbar.

Objective Complete - Mini Debriefing

At this point we can now pick up our torch when we look at it and use it. Once it is in our *inventory* we can then drop it at our position at any time by pressing the *R* key. We've now solved this problem in a specific case; later in this project we will talk about how to solve this for any object that we want to be able to pick up.

Equipping the object

Now, being able to pick up and drop a torch is pretty neat. However, it would be much more exciting to have our player actually move around with the torch in front of the player as if he is holding it.

Engage Thrusters

Thankfully, this is pretty simple to implement.

1. Open up Kismet once again. Create a **Remote Event** action by right-clicking and selecting **New Event | Remote Event**. Inside its Properties window change the **Event Name** value to `Equip`. Create a new object variable (by right-clicking and selecting **Create New Object Variable**) in order to place in the **Instigator** position.

2. To the right-hand side of the **Remote Event "Equip"** action, create a **Set Physics** action by right-clicking and selecting **New Action | Physics | Set Physics**. Inside the action's Properties window change the **new Physics** value to `PHYS_Interpolating`. Connect the **Target** section of the **Set Physics** action to the object that will become the Instigator of the **Remote Event "Equip"** action. Now connect the **Out** output from the **Remove Event "Equip"** action to the **In** input of the **Set Physics** action.

3. To the right-hand side of the **Set Physics** action, create an **Attach to Actor** action by right-clicking and selecting **New Action | Actor | Attach to Actor**. In the object's Properties window check **Use Relative Offset**. After that, set the values of the **X** and **Y** fields to `100` and `-50` in the **Relative Offset** section. Under **Target** create a **Player** variable by right-clicking and selecting **New Variable | Player | Player**, and unchecking the **All Players** option in the Properties window. Connect the **Attachment** section to the same **Instigator** section from the previous step. Connect the **Out** output of the **Set Physics** action to the **In** input of the **Attach to Actor** action.

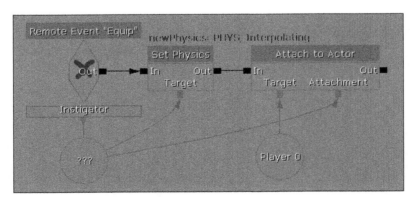

4. After that, create a copy of all of the sequence objects and variables associated with the **Remote Event** action by holding down *Ctrl + Alt* and by clicking and dragging them all. Copy the sequence by pressing *Ctrl + C*, then paste it by pressing *Ctrl + V*. Drag the newly created sequence below the **Remote Event** action.

5. Inside the Properties window of our newly created **Remote Event** action, change the **Event Name** value to Unequip. In the new **Set Physics** action's Properties window change the **new Physics** value to PHYS_RigidBody. Finally in the **Attach to Actor** action check the **Detach** option.

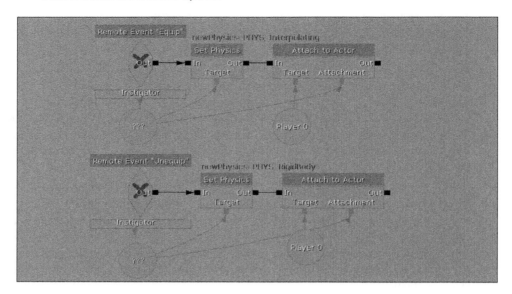

6. To the right-hand side of the **Toggle** action that turns on the **Key Pressed Event** functionality, create an **Activate Remote Event** action by right-clicking and selecting **New Action | Event | Activate Remote Event**. Under the **Event Name** section put Equip. Under the **Instigator** section create an object variable with our torch to connect to it.

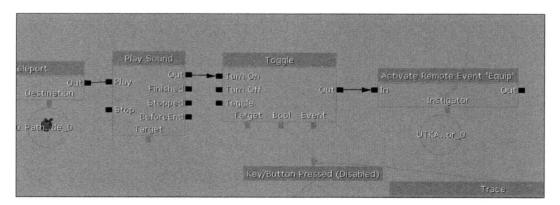

7. In a similar way, to the right-hand side of the **Toggle** action that turns off the **Key Pressed Event** functionality, create an **Activate Remote Event** action by right-clicking and selecting **New Action | Event | Activate Remote Event**. Under the **Event Name** section put `Unequip`. Under the **Instigator** section create an object variable with our torch to connect to it.

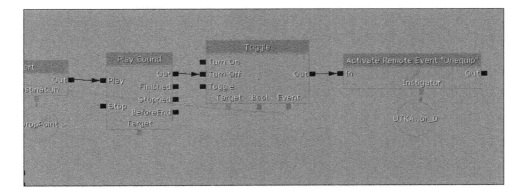

8. Save your project (**File | Save All**) and start your game by pressing *F8* or selecting **Play | In Editor** on the main toolbar.

Objective Complete - Mini Debriefing

At this point, we can now pick up our torch when we look at it and now when we pick it up, it's in our player's hand following the player throughout the world. We can also drop the torch in the same way simply by pressing the *R* key.

Mission Accomplished

Now we have created all of the functionality that is expected of a dynamic object in a game. We can pick it up, we can carry it around, we can drop it, and we can hold it in our hands. Here's one more look at the awesome stuff we accomplished!

You Ready to go Gung HO? A Hotshot Challenge

Through this project, we have learned how to create a dynamic object within a short period of time, but there are still plenty of things we can do! How about you take some time between projects and try to complete the following:

▸ Right now, the torch will currently go through walls. A simple solution would be to use a DynamicBlockingVolume attached to the torch, which I toggle on only when the player is equipping the torch.

▸ Another solution for the same problem is extending the player's collision. Once you are familiar with UnrealScript come back and do that to replace the BlockingVolume.

▸ Create other types of object using the same framework. With minimal work it would be fairly easy to create your own weapons, such as swords, guns, and other carryable objects without having to use UnrealScript, which is something that would be useful to designers who are trying to get their point across before spending time implementing it in code.

Project 7
Managing Loot

We now have an exciting foundation from the previous project in having an object that has the ability to interact with the environment. Now we need some way to manage the objects that we collect.

Thankfully, we have created a rudimentary HUD in *Project 4, Creating a Custom HUD*, using Scaleform with minimal usage of the Kismet Editor. In order to manage our inventory, we could make use of this tool with a deeper understanding of what is going on inside of it.

Let's take our Western-style RPG a step further by creating a rudimentary inventory, expanding on what we have already done, making use of the environment we created in the previous project!

Mission Briefing

In this project, we will create a custom inventory system, making use of a lot of neat features that Flash has that should be able to help you in this project. I'll also provide tips and tools that you can use in your own projects.

This inventory system will allow us to pick up multiple objects and either equip the player with them or drop them on the ground.

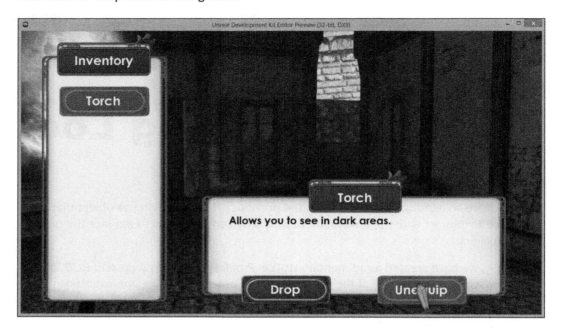

Why Is It Awesome?

The UDK's default inventory system leaves much to be desired and doesn't fit in games that don't have a sci-fi setting. After this project, we will have the makings of an inventory system made from scratch in our own style. We will also have a much greater understanding of Scaleform and just how useful it can be to us.

Your Hotshot Objectives

As usual, we will be following a simple step-by-step process from the beginning to the end to complete the project. Here is an outline of our tasks:

- ▸ Adding a cursor
- ▸ Customizing buttons and resizing windows
- ▸ Building/adding functionalities to the inventory
- ▸ Importing Flash files into the UDK

Mission Checklist

This mission assumes that you have completed the previous three projects or at least are comfortable with what was done in it, as them is built on what we have covered previously.

That being said, Scaleform does not require us to use Adobe Flash, but it is the environment that we will be using to create our UI content. I will be using the latest Adobe Flash CS6, but it is possible to do most of the things in this project using a previous version. For those without Flash, Adobe offers a free trial of all their software. For more information on that, please visit www.adobe.com/go/tryflash/.

We will also need the art assets for our menu. These can be downloaded from the support page on Packt Publishing's website at www.packtpub.com/support.

Adding a cursor

Now for the moment we have all been waiting for—creating our inventory!

Prepare for Lift Off

At this point, I will assume that you have run Adobe Flash CS6 at least once beforehand. If not, you can skip this section to where we actually import the .swf file into the UDK. Alternatively, you can try to use some other way to create a Flash animation to use with the UDK, such as FlashDevelop, Flash Builder, or SlickEdit, but that will have to be done on your own.

Engage Thrusters

Carry out the following steps to add a cursor:

1. Inside Adobe Flash's main menu, create a new ActionScript 3.0 project by going to **Create New | ActionScript 3.0**.

2. In the **PROPERTIES** section of the **Properties** inspector, set the **Size** value to `1280` x `720` by clicking on the existing numbers and typing in the new values and hitting *Enter*. Above the stage, find the zoom scaling that currently says **50%**, as shown in the following screenshot, and change it so that you can see everything within the white box.

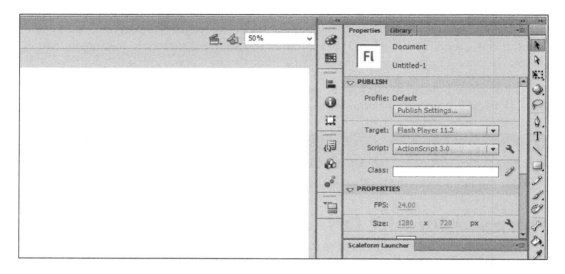

3. If you look at the tabs on the top of the previous screenshot, you will notice that it is on the **Properties** tab. Access the **Library** section by clicking on the tab next to the **Properties** tab.

4. Outside Flash, go to the project's `assets` folder.

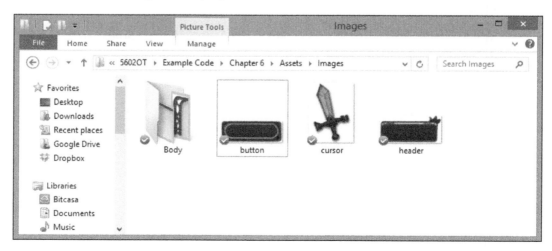

5. Select all of the image files apart from the `Body` folder, and drag-and-drop them into the **Library** tab. Wait for the import dialog to finish and you should see all of the files placed there. Once that is finished, click on the folder icon inside of Flash to create a new folder; give it the name `Body`. Once you do that, open up the `Body` folder and put the nine images of it in there.

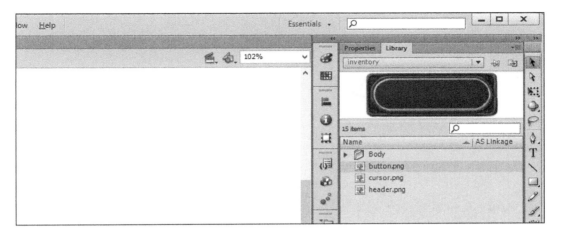

6. From there, go to the **Timeline** section at the bottom of the screen and create a new layer by either clicking on the new layer button on the very bottom-left corner of the program or by right-clicking on **Layer1** and selecting **New Layer**. Double-click on the layer on the top and change its name to `Actionscript`. Double-click on the other layer and give it the name `Inventory`. Create a layer above **Inventory** with the name `Overlay`. You can drag-and-drop layers to put them where you want them.

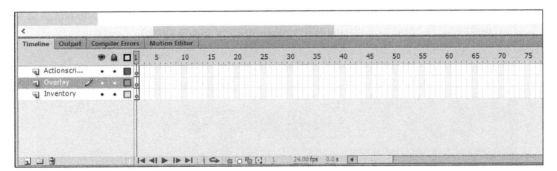

7. Click on the first keyframe of the **Overlay** layer. Drag-and-drop the `cursor.png` file onto the center of the stage.

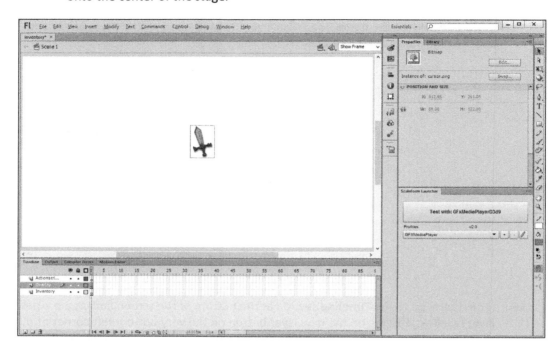

8. Now we need to turn our new cursor image into a movie clip. Click to select and then right-click on the cursor and select **Convert to Symbol...** (alternatively, you can use *F8*). Then, in the **Name** section, type in `Cursor` and confirm that the **Type** value is **Movie Clip**. Once that is set, click on **OK**. Now click on the cursor movie clip, and on the right-hand side change the instance name of the clip to `cursor`.

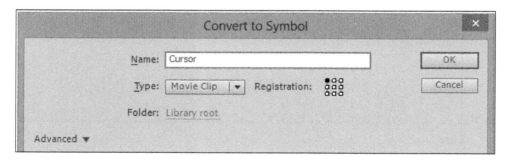

9. Double-click on the cursor to enter its space. At this point, you should see a **+** sign on the top-left corner of the following screenshot. This is where the position of the object will be based. Since we are using this as our mouse cursor, let's move the image in such a way that the tip of the sword is on it, by holding down the left mouse button and dragging it till it is in the position, as shown in the following screenshot:

 To help see the larger picture of things in your Flash file, you may press *F4* in order to toggle the visibility of all of the menus.

10. Double-click on the stage in order to exit the symbol-editing mode. Right-click on the first frame of the **Actionscript** layer and select **Actions**.

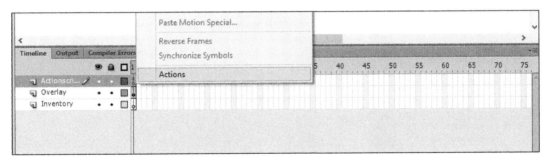

11. There will be a new window that pops up, and it looks like you can write code in it. Every time Flash comes to this frame, it will execute the following code. With that in mind, let's add some new functionality here. Inside the box, on the right-hand side put the following code:

```
// Whenever the mouse moves, we call the mousePosition
// function
stage.addEventListener(MouseEvent.MOUSE_MOVE,
mousePosition);

function mousePosition(event:MouseEvent)
{
  // Set the cursor's position to the mouse's new one.
  cursor.x = mouseX;
  cursor.y = mouseY;
}
```

When you finish, the window should look like it does in the following screenshot:

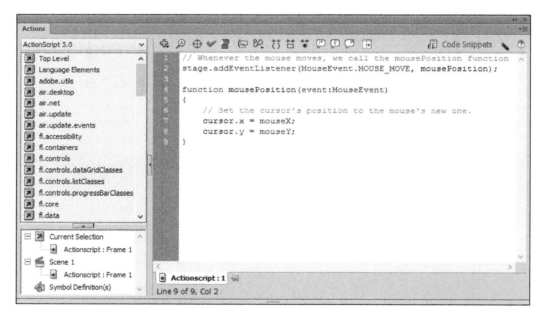

12. Save your project by going to **File | Save**, and type in a name of your choice (I used `hotshot_inventory`). Next, test your project by clicking on the **Test with: GFxMediaPlayerD3d9** button to start up the program.

 Should you not see the Scaleform Launcher, first make sure that you followed the same steps as mentioned in *Project 4, Creating A Custom HUD*, in order to set Flash up for Scaleform development. If you have not, you can always find it by going to **Debug | Other Panels | Scaleform Launcher**.

Objective Complete - Mini Debriefing

You can see now that when we move our mouse on the screen, the sword icon moves along with us! This will be quite useful at any point when the user would like to use the mouse.

Customizing buttons and resizing windows

When working with an inventory of any kind, being as adjustable as possible is a very good stance to take, as many things are going to be iterated on as the game is play-tested. Being able to resize objects without having to recreate art assets is a very valuable tool.

We may also require to introduce functionality that currently doesn't exist in objects.

Engage Thrusters

One way we can be sure our objects will have the functionality that we want is to create classes of our own. But first, let's add in some graphical content!

1. On the right-hand side of Flash in the **Library** tab, right-click and select **New Symbol**. Once there, in the **Name** section type in `InvBody` and confirm that the **Type** value is **Movie Clip**. Click on the **Advanced** tab and check the **Enable guides for 9-slice scaling** and **Export for ActionScript** options; then press **OK**.

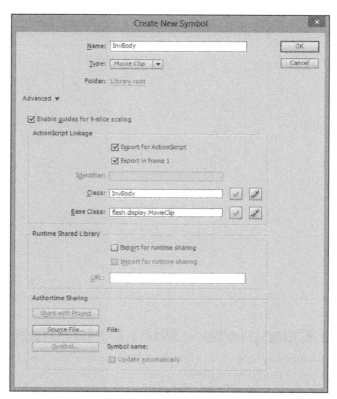

2. Double-click on the newly created movie clip to enter it. You will notice four dotted lines.

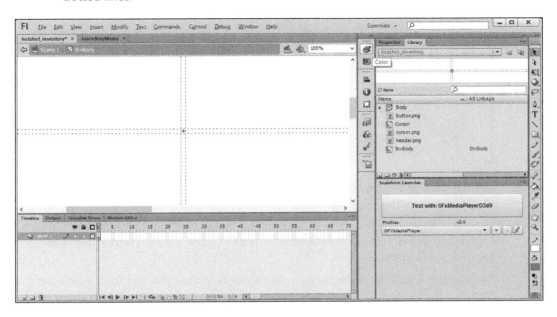

3. Drag-and-drop the nine images from the Body folder into this movie clip, fitting them together. The images go from the top-left corner to the right-hand corner, and then move down to the next row while maintaining three images for each row. After placing the images, drag the grid lines to fit the images between them.

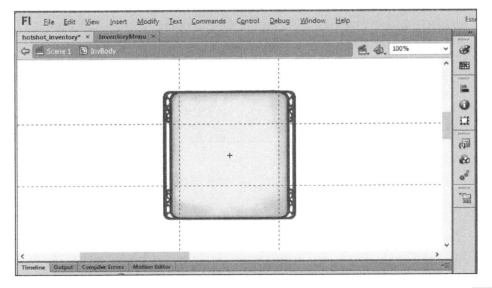

What this will do is anytime we create a body and change the width and height, the four non-cardinal corners will not scale but the others will, allowing us to create boxes of whatever size we want. Pretty nifty, huh?

4. Click on the arrow point to the left-hand side on the top bar to exit this movie clip and go back to the stage. Right-click on the **Library** tab and create another movie clip with the name `myButton`. In the **Advanced** tab, check **Export for ActionScript**.

Flash has its own button that you can use in your projects. However, having a button class in our project allows us to customize it the way we want and create a custom functionality for the customized button.

5. Double-click on the **myButton** movie clip in order to enter it. Create two layers inside of it, with the upper named `Actionscript` and the lower named `Button`.

6. Drag-and-drop the `button.png` file into this movie clip. Right-click on it and select **Convert to Symbol**. In the **Name** section, type in `buttonBack`; under the **Type** section, set **Graphic**.

7. Click on the **T** button on the far right-hand side to access the Text tool. Inside the frame of the button, click and drag to create a place to enter text. Experiment with the **CHARACTER** settings until you find something you like. I personally used **Century Gothic** in the **Family** section, and also used **Bold** with the **Size** value set to `32`.

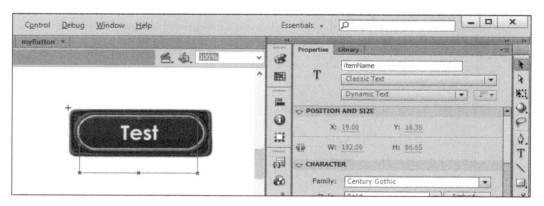

8. Next to the **Style** option, there is a button that says **Embed**. Click on it to access the **Font Embedding** menu. In the **Options** tab, check the **Uppercase**, **Lowercase**, and **Numerals** options. Then go to the **ActionScript** tab and check the **Export for ActionScript** and **Export in Frame 1** options; now hit the **OK** button.

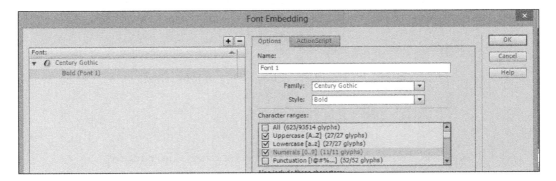

 Scaleform works better with some fonts than with others, and it may not be apparent until you get into the UDK; so when working with fonts, try to make sure it works before working too much with a particular font.

9. Click on the first frame to access the frame's Properties window. On the right-hand side, change the value of **Label** to base. Create two new keyframes with the labels hover and selected.

10. On each of the three frames, open up the **Actions** box (right-click on the frame and select **Actions**) and put the following code into each of them:

```
// By default text blocks the mouse, this disables that
itemName.mouseEnabled = false;

    // Do not move to the next frame
stop();
```

11. Next, go into the myButton script file by right-clicking on it in the **Library** tab and then clicking on the pencil icon next to the **Class** option in the **ActionScript Linkage** section. If it asks which application to open, just hit **OK**.

12. Once inside the file, replace the code with the following code snippet:

```
package {
   importflash.display.MovieClip;
   importflash.events.MouseEvent;

   public class myButton extends MovieClip
   {
```

```
// Variables that will be used by ourButton Class
varmyButtonName:String = "";
vardesc:String = "";
varitemDesc = "";

// Constructor - Gets called when this object is
                created
public function myButton()
{
  this.addEventListener(MouseEvent.MOUSE_OVER,
                        mouseHover);
  this.gotoAndStop("base");
}

// mouseHover - When the mouse is over the button,
// play the hover animation.
function mouseHover (e:MouseEvent):void{
  this.gotoAndStop("hover");
  this.removeEventListener(MouseEvent.MOUSE_OVER,
                           mouseHover);
  this.addEventListener(MouseEvent.MOUSE_OUT,
                        mouseNormal);
  this.addEventListener(MouseEvent.MOUSE_DOWN,
                        mouseSelected);
}

// mouseSelected - When the mouse clicks the item he
// wants to use it. Toggle being selected.
function mouseSelected (e:MouseEvent):void{
  this.gotoAndStop("selected");
  this.removeEventListener(MouseEvent.MOUSE_OVER,
                           mouseHover);
  this.removeEventListener(MouseEvent.MOUSE_OUT,
                           mouseNormal);
  this.removeEventListener(MouseEvent.MOUSE_DOWN,
                           mouseSelected);

  // If we select it again we unselect the item
  this.addEventListener(MouseEvent.MOUSE_DOWN,
```

```
                              mouseNormal);
}

// mouseNormal - The button's normal state.
function mouseNormal (e:MouseEvent):void {
  this.gotoAndStop("base");
  this.addEventListener(MouseEvent.MOUSE_OVER,
                        mouseHover);
  this.removeEventListener(MouseEvent.MOUSE_OUT,
                           mouseNormal);
  this.removeEventListener(MouseEvent.MOUSE_DOWN,
                           mouseSelected);
}
}
```

This is depicted in the following screenshot:

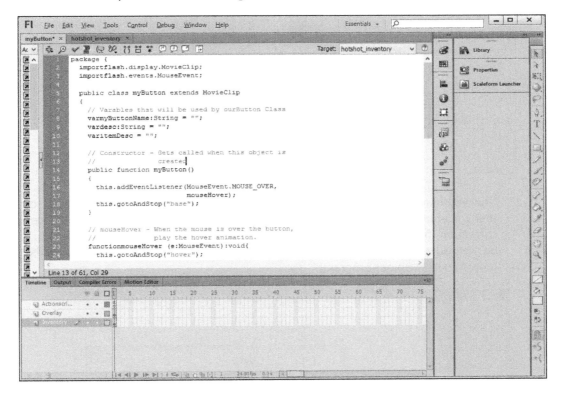

13. Save the file by pressing *Ctrl + S*.

14. Go back to the `hotshot_inventory.fla` file once again by clicking on its tab at the top. Click on the **Timeline** tab and then click on the first frame of the **Inventory** layer. Drag-and-drop the **InvBody** movie clip from the **Properties** section onto the stage (where we've been placing objects previously). Access its Properties window by clicking on the object with the **Properties** tab selected; then enter `425` for the **X** value and `550` for the **Y** value. Change the **W** (width) value to `700` and **H** (height) to `256`.

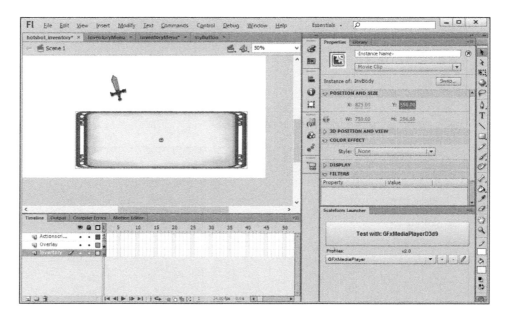

15. Now you may be thinking, "Wait, I thought the reason we did the grid thing was so that we would not see things all stretchy." And yes, you are correct: it does not look correct on the editor side of things, but I assure you that when we run it you will be pleased with the results. Now, try pressing the **Test with: GFxMediaPlayerD3d9** button to start up our program.

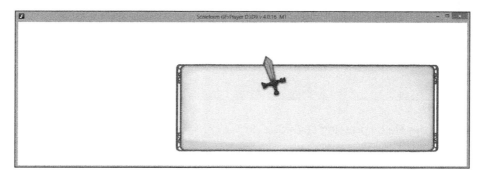

Objective Complete - Mini Debriefing

Once the game starts, you will notice that not only does the body look pretty sharp, but our cursor is also above our object with no issues. Pretty nifty, and the perfect base for building our inventory. Enabling the nine-scale grid has made it possible for Flash to use the three images on the top and three on the bottom at their normal size. It will then scale the rows on the left and right sides of the grid using the y axis and will scale the center row to fit the space that's left, enabling a clean-looking menu that we can easily use to create images at our preferred size.

Building/adding functionality to the inventory

We now have all of the building blocks that we need in order to create our entire HUD.

Engage Thrusters

With that in mind, let's get building!

1. Drag-and-drop two **myButton** buttons onto the stage while still being in the **InvBody** movie clip, placing them on the bottom of the inventory box in the way shown in the following screenshot. Make sure the **Properties** tab is selected on the top-right corner. In their properties, give one the instance name `equipButton` and the other the instance name `dropButton`.

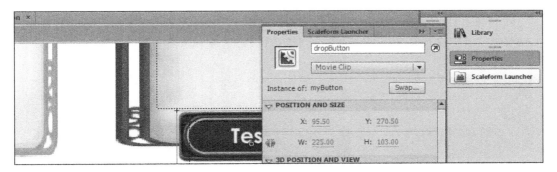

2. Drag-and-drop the `header.png` object to the top of our **InvBody** movie clip (like the following screenshot). Then create a new text field with the label `infoHeader`. This will change to be whatever object we have selected: I have put the text `Torch` as its instance name.

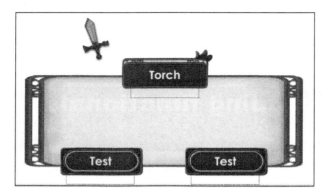

3. Next, we need to create a text field to hold the description of the object we have, in exactly the same way that we have been creating text by selecting the Text tool and then dragging-and-dropping to create a box in which we can put text. Access the newly created textbox's Properties window and give it the label `desc`. I personally used the same font with a **Size** value of `26`.

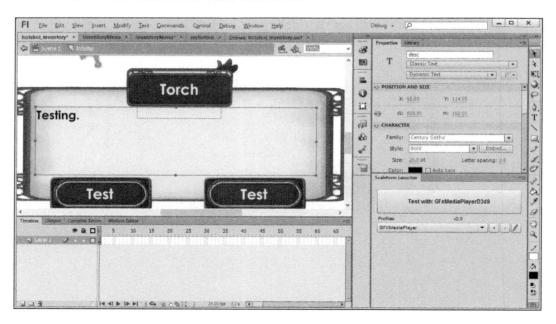

4. Now hold down *Shift* and select all of the objects that we just created, except the sword. Then right-click and select **Convert To Symbol** and make it a movie clip called `InfoBar`. Then, once it has been created, change the instance name to `infoBar`.

5. Now, we need to create a holder for all of the items we will collect. Let's do that now. Drag another **InvBody** movie clip over to the left-hand side of the stage. Scale it much more in the vertical direction than we did before. You can do this either by typing in numbers or using the Transform tool (*Ctrl* + *T*).

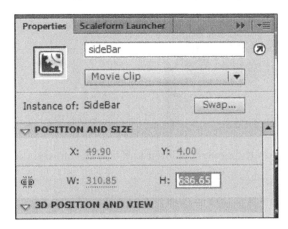

6. When you are finished, put another header in; but this time, actually put the text `Inventory` in it as we will not be modifying it at runtime.

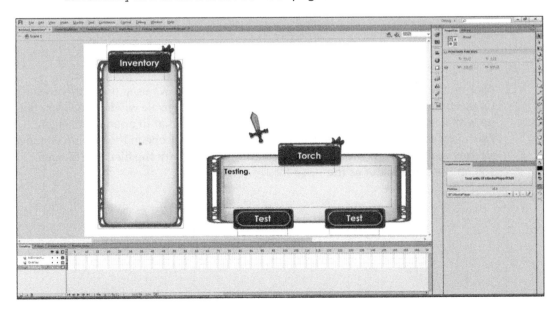

7. Convert all of the inventory objects on the left-hand side to a movie clip called `SideBar`; then give it the instance name `sideBar`.

8. Click on the stage once again and access the **Properties** inspector. Under the **PUBLISH** section in the **Class** field, type in the name you saved the file with.

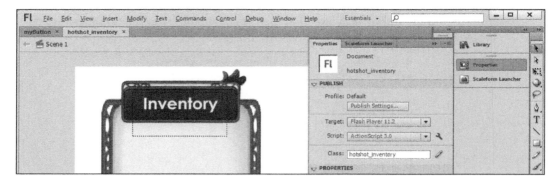

9. After that, click on the pencil beside it and you should see the following warning:

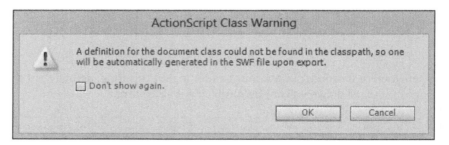

10. With that in mind, let's export the project!

11. Click on the **Test with: GFxMediaPlayerD3d9** button that we used previously to start up our program. After it has run, close it as well as the console window that opened up with it. Click on the pencil icon again and it may ask what to open with. Select **Flash Professional** and click on **OK**. You should see some code in the pop-up window already written for us. Save that file (by hitting *Ctrl + S*) with the filename given to you, in the same folder as the `.fla` file.

12. Replace the text in the file with the following code snippet. Rather than giving little snippets at a time to understand how the code works, the entire sequence is given to read through. The code is well commented, explaining what is going on throughout.

> If you face problems with understanding this code, please take some time to read *Project 8, UnrealScript: A Primer*, which uses a different programming language, but has a lot of the same principles and goes at a very slow pace.

```
package  {

    import flash.display.MovieClip;
    import flash.events.KeyboardEvent;
    import flash.events.MouseEvent;
    import myButton; /* Our own created class */

    import scaleform.gfx.Extensions;
    import flash.system.fscommand;

    public class hotshot_inventory extends MovieClip
    {

        // Initial placement of inventory items and spacing
        public static var inventoryYPlacement:int = 135.85;
        public static var inventoryXPlacement:int = 42;
        public static var spaceBetweenItemsY:int = 100;

        // An object that will contain all items in our
        // inventory
        public static var inventory:Array = [];

        /* Helper variables */
        public var itemToDrop:String = "";
        public var itemToEquip:String = "";
        public var itemToDropNumber:int = 0;
        public static var showDetails:Boolean = false;
```

This code outlines the variables that we want to use throughout our inventory. We will be using these variables in both Unreal and Flash so that our inventory acts the same on both sides.

```
/**********************************************************
       Function:   hotshot_inventory (Constructor)

    Description:   Called when this object is created.
                   Contains functionality of our inventory
                   class.

        Inputs:   None
       Outputs:   None
**********************************************************/
    public function hotshot_inventory() {
    // Enable Scaleform
    Extensions.enabled = true;

    // We want to be able to drop and equip stuff.
    stage.addEventListener(KeyboardEvent.KEY_DOWN,
    keyhit);
    infoBar.dropButton.addEventListener(MouseEvent.MOUSE_
    DOWN, dropSelected);
    infoBar.equipButton.addEventListener(MouseEvent.MOUSE_
    DOWN, equipSelected);
    infoBar.dropButton.myButtonName = "Drop";
    infoBar.dropButton.itemName.text = "Drop";
    infoBar.equipButton.myButtonName = "Equip";
    infoBar.equipButton.itemName.text = "Equip";

    // Just as an FYI, if you want to do any debugging,
    // you can create items in the inventory in the
    // following way:
    // addInventory("ItemName","Description");

    // Until the user taps 'I' to enter the inventory they
    // will not see the inventory.
    sideBar.visible = false;
    cursor.visible = false;
    infoBar.visible = false;
    cursor.mouseEnabled = false;
    }
```

This code is typically known as a constructor. Normally, this will initialize any values that we need to set, and for setting up events that you want to use when an object is placed on a stage. Since this is our base class, it will be called when the program starts.

```
/*********************************************************
     Function:   dropSelected / equipSelected
  Description:   Event that actually calls the function
                 that we want to use (dropItem/equipItem)
                 with the correct parameters.

      Inputs:   event - MouseEvent needed to add the
                Event Listener
     Outputs:   None
 *********************************************************/
function dropSelected(event:MouseEvent):void {
  dropItem(getSelectedInventory().myButtonName);
}

function equipSelected(event:MouseEvent):void {
  equipItem(getSelectedInventory().myButtonName);
}
```

These two functions call the appropriate method when either the equip or drop buttons are clicked.

```
/*********************************************************
     Function:   dropItem

  Description:   Will drop an item that is currently
                 selected from the player's inventory.
                 If equipped, it will first unequip it
                 before dropping.

      Inputs:   itemName - the name of the item we want
                to remove.

     Outputs:   None
 *********************************************************/
  public function dropItem(itemName:String)
  {
   itemToDrop = itemName;
   // If the item is equipped, we need to unequip it by
   // calling equipItem again.
    if(itemToDrop == itemToEquip)
    {
```

```
      equipItem(itemName);
   }
   // Remove the item from the inventory
   removeInventory(itemName);

   // We no longer need to see the info screen
   showDetails = false;
   infoBar.visible = false;

   //Tell UDK that we dropped something
   fscommand('dropItem');
}


/**********************************************************
   Function:     equipItem

Description:     Will equip an item that is currently
                 selected from the player's inventory as
                 long as nothing else is already equipped.
                 If the item is equipped twice it will
                 unequip it.

    Inputs:      itemName - the name of the item we want
                 to remove.

   Outputs:      None
**********************************************************/

public function equipItem(itemName:String)
{
   // Have we equipped anything yet?
   if(itemToEquip == "")
   {
      itemToEquip = itemName;
      //Tell UDK that we are equipping an item
      fscommand('equipItem');
      infoBar.equipButton.gotoAndStop("selected");
   }
   else
   {
     //Check if player wants to unequip
     if(itemName == itemToEquip)
     {
        //Tell UDK that we are unequipping an item
        fscommand('unequipItem');
```

```
                    itemToEquip = "";
                }
            }
        }
```

These two functions do the actual picking up and dropping. Note that the
fscommand function is actually telling the UDK to call an event that we will
create in Kismet in the next task.

```
    /************************************************************
    Function:     keyHit

    Description:  Registers if the player is trying access
                  the inventory and will toggle visibility
                  of everything.

        Inputs:   e - the KeyboardEvent that contains all
                  what keys are currently being pressed and
                  used.

        Outputs:  None
    ************************************************************/
    private function keyhit(e:KeyboardEvent):void
    {
        if(e.keyCode == 73) /* 73 is the 'I' key */
        {
            sideBar.visible = !sideBar.visible;
            cursor.visible = !cursor.visible;

            if(sideBar.visible)
            {
                fscommand('usingInventory');
            }
            else
            {
                infoBar.visible = false;
                fscommand('finishedInventory');
            }
            if(sideBar.visible && showDetails)
            {
                infoBar.visible = true
            }
        }
    }
```

This will toggle the visibility of our inventory whenever our player presses the *I* key. This can actually be set to whatever value you like, and you can actually extend this to work with whatever kind of functionality that you like. Note that we call an `fscommand` function when we start using the inventory and when we're done using it.

```
/**********************************************************
    Function:     addInventory

    Description:  Adds a new item to our inventory.
                  Called from Kismet.

       Inputs:    itemName - name of the object being
                  added. desc - the description of the
                  item being added.

      Outputs:    None
**********************************************************/
public function addInventory(itemName:String,
                             desc:String = "")
{
  // Create a new button with the details of the item.
    var button:myButton = new myButton();
    button.x = inventoryXPlacement;
    button.y = inventoryYPlacement +
               spaceBetweenItemsY * inventory.length;
    button.desc = desc;
    button.myButtonName = itemName;
    button.itemName.text = itemName;
    sideBar.addChild(button);
    inventory.push(button);
}
```

This adds an item to our inventory that we can then equip or drop within UDK. We also added a button to our actual inventory. This is a function that is actually called from Kismet.

```
/**********************************************************
    Function:     removeInventory

    Description:  Removes an item from our inventory.

       Inputs:    itemName - name of the object being
                  removed.

      Outputs:    None
**********************************************************/
```

```
public function removeInventory(itemName:String)
{
  var deleted:Boolean = false;
  var i:int = 0;
  for (i = 0; i < inventory.length; i++)
  {
    var book:myButton = inventory[i];
    if(!deleted)
    {
      // If we find the correct item
      if(book.myButtonName == itemName)
      {
        // Remove the button from the
        // inventory and world.
        inventory.splice(i, 1);
        book.gotoAndStop(1);
        book.parent.removeChild(book);
        // We found it, no need to continue
        // searching
        deleted = true;

        // Item is dropped
        itemToDrop = "";
      }
    }
  }
}
```

This function will actually remove an item from our inventory in both Unreal and our Flash file. This function will also be called from the UDK to fix our inventory on this end.

```
/*********************************************************

   Function:     getSelectedInventory

   Description:  Returns to us the object that is
                 currently selected in the inventory
                 (if any).

      Inputs:    None

     Outputs:    book - the object in the inventory
                 that is currently selected (last
                 clicked on)
*********************************************************/
```

```
public function getSelectedInventory():myButton
{
  for each (var book:myButton in inventory)
{
    // check if the button is in the frame
    // labeled "selected" (the third frame)
    if(book.currentFrame == 3)
    {
      //return the object
      return book;
    }
  }
  //If we didn't find anything, return nothing
    return null;
}


} // end of class hotshot_inventory

} // end of package
```

Finally, this function is actually used by other functions in order to make our lives easier. In general, if we have a piece of code that will be used in many places, it's usually better to just create a function based off of it.

13. Now, go back into our myButton class by opening our myButton.as file. At the very top, insert the import hotshot_inventory; line. This will give us access to the properties of the document class.

14. Now, replace the mouseSelected function with the following code:

```
// mouseSelected - When the mouse clicks the item he
// wants to use it. Toggles being selected.
functionmouseSelected (e:MouseEvent):void {
if(myButtonName == "Drop")
  {
return;
  }
if((myButtonName != "Equip") && (myButtonName != "Holding") &&
(myButtonName != "Unequip"))
  {
    // If we select it again we unselect the item
      varprevSelected:myButton;

prevSelected = hotshot_inventory(
root).getSelectedInventory();
```

```
if(prevSelected != null)
    {
prevSelected.mouseNormal(e);
    }

    // The object is now selected until we choose
    // something else.
this.gotoAndStop("selected");
itemName.text = myButtonName;

    // Being selected, it doesn't need to have
    // interactions with the mouse
this.removeEventListener(MouseEvent.MOUSE_OVER,
mouseHover);
this.removeEventListener(MouseEvent.MOUSE_OUT,
mouseNormal);
this.removeEventListener(MouseEvent.MOUSE_DOWN,
mouseSelected);

  // Have our inventory show it being selected. Set the
  // infoBar's data
hotshot_inventory.showDetails = true;
hotshot_inventory(root).infoBar.visible = true;
hotshot_inventory(root).infoBar.infoHeader.text =
myButtonName;
hotshot_inventory(root).infoBar.desc.text =  desc;
  }

  // If we are holding the item, we can unequip it
if(hotshot_inventory(root).itemToEquip ==
hotshot_inventory(root).getSelectedInventory().itemName.text)
  {
hotshot_inventory(root).infoBar.equipButton.myButtonName
    = "Unequip";
hotshot_inventory(root).infoBar.equipButton.itemName.text
    = "Unequip";
  }
  //If you're not holding anything, you can equip it
else if (hotshot_inventory(root).itemToEquip == "")
  {
hotshot_inventory(root).infoBar.equipButton.myButtonName
    = "Equip";
hotshot_inventory(root).infoBar.equipButton.itemName.text
    = "Equip";
  }
```

```
// Otherwise we're holding something already.
else
{
trace(myButtonName);
hotshot_inventory(root).infoBar.equipButton.myButtonName
    = "Holding";
hotshot_inventory(root).infoBar.equipButton.itemName.text
    = "Holding";

}
}
```

This is depicted in the following screenshot:

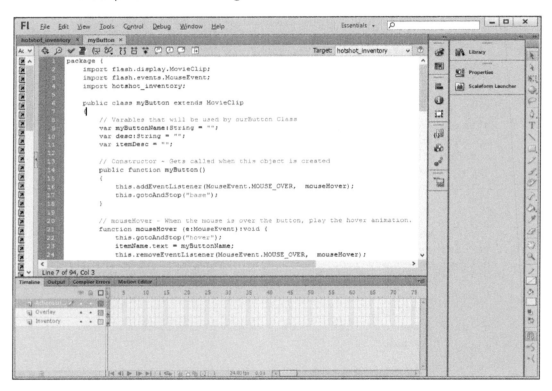

15. Save your project by hitting *Ctrl + S* on both files and then click on the **Test with: GFxMediaPlayerD3d9** button on the Scaleform Launcher to start up our program. Press the *I* key and you should see something cool pop up.

Objective Complete - Mini Debriefing

It was a bit more difficult than before, but we have now created an exciting new inventory system. Let's get it into the UDK so that we can use it!

Importing Flash files into the UDK

Now that we have our content, let's bring it in!

Engage Thrusters

Those who have worked on our previous Scaleform demo know the drill: we now have to do some specific things in order to get our Flash files to play nice with the UDK.

1. The UDK can only import Flash files that are within a specific folder. Inside your file browser, go to the folder with your .fla and .as files. In the folder, you should see a file with a .swf extension (hotshot_inventory.swf). Copy that file and go to your UDK installation folder (UDKGame\Flash\) and create a new folder called Hotshot (if it does not exist already). Inside that folder, paste the .swf Flash movie file.

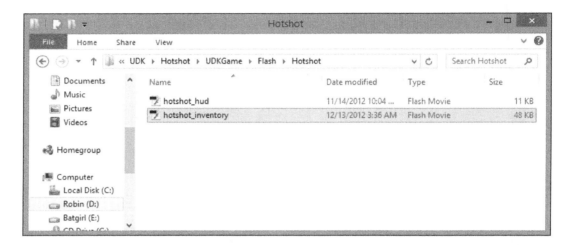

 You may notice the hotshot_hud.swf file: it is the project that we created in *Project 4, Creating a Custom HUD*. In this section we will be doing something similar to that.

2. Start up the UDK again. Open up the **Content Browser** window and click on the **Import** button. Find the movie file and select **OK**. You will notice that the **Import** dialog already sets the package name to `Hotshot`, so just say **OK** and save this package. If it asks you to fully load the package, say **OK** to that too.

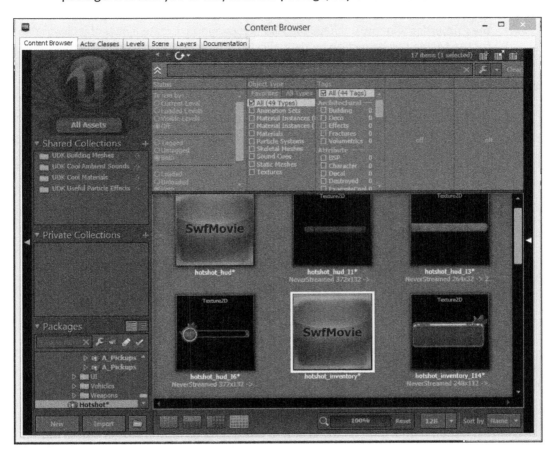

3. With the movie selected, open up Kismet. Create a **Level Loaded** event by right-clicking and going to **New Event | Level Loaded**. To the right-hand side of the **Level Loaded** event, create an **Open GFx Movie** action by right-clicking and going to **New Action | GFx UI | Open GFx Movie**. Create a player variable for the **Player Owner** section by right-clicking and going to **New Variable | Player | Player**, and in the Properties window uncheck the **All Players** option. Create a new object variable for the **Movie Player** section by right-clicking on the pink arrow and selecting **Create New Object Variable**. Click on the action to see its properties, and with the SwfMovie selected in the **Content Browser** window, click on the green arrow in the **Movie** property. Connect **Loaded** and **Visible** from the **Level Loaded** event to the **In** input of the **Open GFx Movie** action.

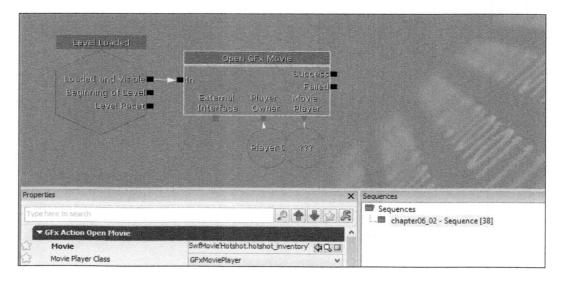

4. Now create an **FsCommand** event by right-clicking and going to **New Event | GFx UI | FsCommand**. Click on the action to see its Properties window, and with the SwfMovie selected in the **Content Browser** window, click on the green arrow in the **Movie** property. Under **FSCommand**, put in `usingInventory`. Create a copy below it and use `finishedInventory` for the **FSCommand** value.

5. In between the two **FSCommand** events, create a **Toggle Cinematic Mode** action by right-clicking and going to **New Action | Toggle | Toggle Cinematic Mode**. Connect the **Out** output of the **FSCommand** action (**usingInventory**) to the **Enable** input of the **Toggle Cinematic Mode** action. Connect the **Out** output of the **FSCommand** action (**finishedInventory**) to the **Disable** input of the **Toggle Cinematic Mode** action.

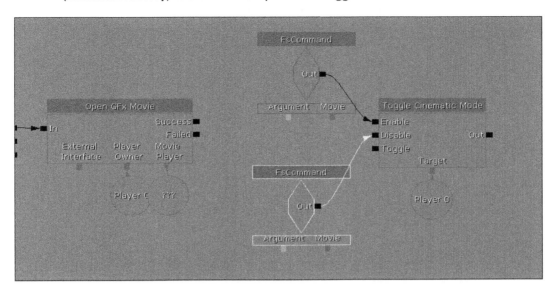

6. Now create another **FsCommand** event by right-clicking and going to **New Event | GFx UI | FsCommand**. Click on the action to see its Properties window, and with the SwfMovie selected in the **Content Browser** window, click on the green arrow in the **Movie** property. Under **FSCommand**, type in `equipItem`.

7. To the right-hand side of the **FSCommand** action, create an **Activate Remote Event** action by right-clicking and going to **New Action | Event | Activate Remote Event**. Under **Event Name**, type in `Equip`. Under **Instigator**, create an object variable with our torch to connect to it. Connect the **Out** output from the **FsCommand** action (**equipItem**) to the **In** input of the **Activate Remote Event "Equip"** action.

8. Duplicate the **FsCommand** event and change the value to unequipItem. In the same way, create a copy of the **Activate Remote Event "Equip"** action, change the **Event Name** value to Unequip, and connect it in the same way as the previous one. Next, connect the **Out** output of the **Activate Remote Event "Unequip"** action to the **In** input of the **Teleport** action, which is to the right-hand side of the **Trigger_Dynamic_1 Used** event.

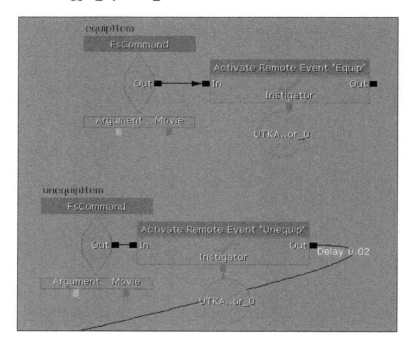

9. Replace the **Key/Button Pressed** event that we associated with the *R* key in *Project 6, Dynamic Loot*, in the *Dropping the object* section, with an **FSCommand** event. This is set up just as we did previously, with an **Event Name** value of dropItem. Also, add a **Delay** value of 0.16 seconds between the **Not Obstructed** section of the **Trace** action and the **In** input of the **Teleport** action by right-clicking on the **In** input and then selecting **Set Activate Delay**.

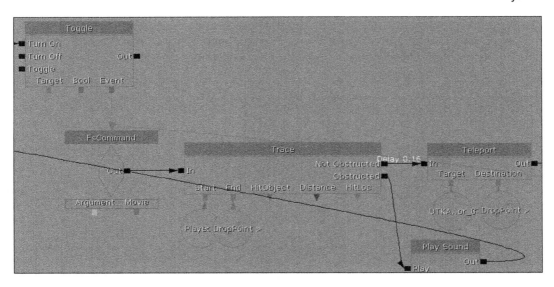

10. Speaking of the **Trigger_Dynamic_1 Used** event, select it and give some space between the two actions by holding down *Alt* and dragging it leftwards. Then remove the connection between the **Used** section of the **Trigger_Dynamic_1 Used** event and the **In** input of the **Teleport** action.

11. Create a **GFx Invoke ActionScript** action by right-clicking and going to **New Action | GFx UI | GFx Invoke ActionScript**. Connect the **Movie Player** section to the **Movie Player** variable of the **GFx Open Movie** action. Inside the Properties window, set the **Method Name** value to `root.addInventory`. In the **Arguments** section, create two parts using the **+** button. Change both of their **Type** values to **AS_String**. Then, in the **S** part type in `Torch` for the first part and `Allows you to see in dark areas` in the second. The following screenshot shows all of these values being set as a reference.

As I pointed out in the `hotshot_inventory.as` file, what this is basically doing is calling the function `addInventory` from the `hotshot_inventory` class with the first argument being the name of the object we are adding, and the second being a description of it. This will make it possible to add whatever kinds of items we want into our game, without having to go to Flash again. Pretty nifty!

12. Finally, connect the **Out** output from the **Play Sound** action connected to the **Obstructed** part of the **Trace** action, to the **In** input of the **GFx Invoke ActionScript** action. This basically means that if we cannot drop the item, we add it back to our inventory.

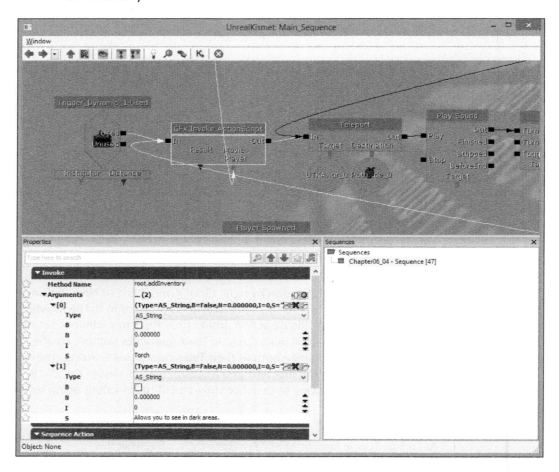

13. Build your project by going to **Build | Build All**. Save your game by going to **File | Save All**, and run your game by selecting **Play | In Editor**.

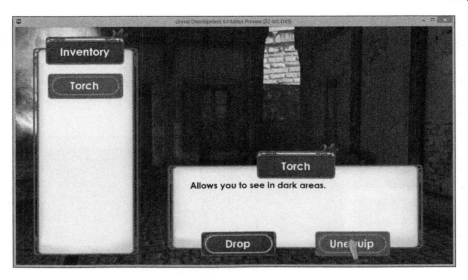

Objective Complete - Mini Debriefing

And with that, we have a pretty awesome inventory in the making, with support on the Flash end for up to five different items at a time (and even more if you add scrollbars on the menu). One of the nice things about Scaleform is the ability to load multiple movies at a time. Bringing in the HUD we created earlier with a slight delay gives us both pieces of the game.

At this point, you have all the tools you need to get started to extend this prototype to whatever you would like to see it become!

Mission Accomplished

With that, we have taken our Scaleform knowledge to the next level and have a much better understanding on how the UDK and Flash can communicate with each other making use of features like the **FSCommand** event and the **GFx Invoke ActionScript** action. Let's take one final look at what we have accomplished:

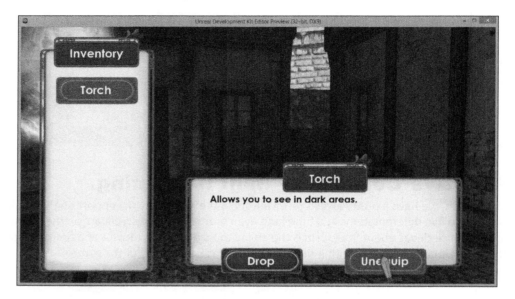

You Ready to go Gung HO? A Hotshot Challenge

Through this project, we have learned how to create a HUD within a short period of time, but there is still plenty of things we can do! How about you take some time between projects and try to complete the following:

- ▶ Bring in the HUD that we created in *Project 4, Creating a Custom HUD,* and adjust the inventory in such a way that it does not cover the HUD we just added.

- ▶ Make the buttons use the `scale9Grid` functionality as well, so you can have items of whatever size you want!

- ▶ Add new objects for the player to pick up and adjust Kismet to handle multiple objects. For those trying to go for a robust system, I would suggest you to look into using object lists, adding the objects as you put them into the inventory with both the Flash file and Unreal having a copy of the data that they need, to work correctly.

Project 8
UnrealScript: A Primer

We have learned about many things that are not covered very much elsewhere, but to truly exploit UDK to its fullest potential, you will have to use UnrealScript.

UnrealScript (also known as **Uscript**) is a programming language designed and developed by Epic Games as a way for people to make it possible to modify what the Unreal Engine does without recompiling the engine's source code that was made in C++. In this way, it is similar to a scripting language such as Lua, C#, or Python; however, it is not a scripting or interpreted language because of the fact that you have to actually compile UnrealScript in order for changes to be made.

For those familiar with object-oriented programming, UnrealScript should not be too difficult to pick up, as most functionality is based on expanding code that is already written, but I am sure that the majority of you, for the most part, have only touched on the features of UDK and are interested in learning more. If that is the case, this project is for you!

Mission Briefing

In this project, we will first gain an understanding of when to use UnrealScript for applications. We will then set up some tools to help us gain an understanding of the code that Epic provided and give some guidance on how object-oriented programming works. After that, we will learn how to install the IDE and write a simple "Hello world!" object. Then after that, we will move on to create another more complicated object with a dynamically flickering light!

The book does not display it too well, but the following screenshot is of that flashing light in action:

Why Is It Awesome?

After this project, you should have the fundamental knowledge to go out and create your own custom game types, objects, characters, and weapons within UDK.

Your Hotshot Objectives

As usual, we will be following a simple step-by-step process from the beginning to the end to complete the project. Here is an outline of our tasks:

- ▸ Installing UnCodeX
- ▸ Setting up our IDE
- ▸ Writing "Hello world" in UnrealScript
- ▸ Creating a flickering light object

Mission Checklist

This mission assumes that you have UDK installed and have some familiarity with it. No other previous knowledge is required.

Installing UnCodeX

For newcomers and veteran programmers, reading someone else's code is often the major part of your job; after all you do not want to rewrite something that is already provided to you (unless you have a reason to do so).

Having an understanding of the code base you are working is paramount to writing code that does not conflict with stuff that is written. In order to help you when starting out, I have a tool, which you can use in your daily workflow to make your life much easier, called UnCodeX.

Written by Michiel "El Muerte" Hendriks, UnCodeX can create a class and a package tree from the UnrealScript sources, and analyze the content of each class for later use.

UnCodeX organizes more than 2,000 files that are located within our UDK's `Development\ Src` folder and displays them in a way that makes it easy to see relationships between classes.

UnCodeX also gives you the ability to create a highly detailed HTML API reference from your code. It includes all definitions made in classes, syntax-highlighted source code, links to the type declarations, and automatic JavaDoc-like documentation from your source code. Those who have used Doxygen should feel right at home here.

Engage Thrusters

Here are the steps to download and install UnCodeX:

1. First, open up a web browser of your choice (I personally use Chrome) and go to `http://sourceforge.net/projects/uncodex/`. Once there, click on the green **Download** button.

2. Once it has finished downloading, double-click on the `UnCodeX-v241-setup.exe` file in your `Downloads` folder.

3. Go through the installer and when you are finished, make sure the **Launch UnCodeX** option is selected and then select **Finish**.

4. You will then get a pop-up dialog box asking to change the settings; select **Yes**.

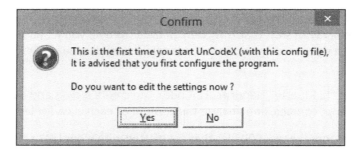

5. At this point, the UnCodeX window will pop up with the **Source Paths** tab selected. Click on the **Add** button, select the `Development\Src` folder within your UDK installation path, and then select **OK**. After this, click on the **Yes** button on the dialog box that asks us to scan the directory.

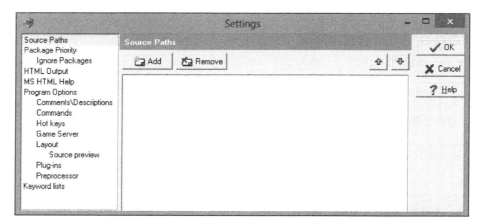

6. At this point, you should see UnCodeX scan and organize all of the files within our folder and display them for us to see and enjoy.

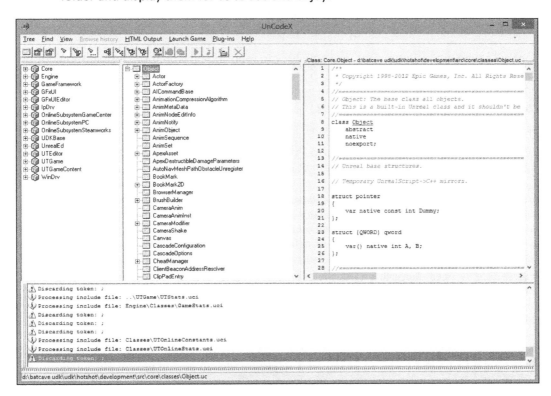

Objective Complete - Mini Debriefing

UnCodeX has now been configured properly and is available for us to use!

Classified Intel

Now, let's go over what UnCodeX is actually showing us and what we can use it for.

The window on the left-hand side shows packages in our source and the classes contained in them. A package acts similarly to a folder in Windows in that it holds things that can be used. We have actually already used packages whenever we imported new content to our projects.

In the middle, you will see the class tree, which organizes all of the objects based on their relationship to each other. You will see at the very top the Object class. This class is inherited by all other objects in UDK, which means every object that is inherited has all of the data and functionality that its parent has. All classes must be inherited from another class, with the exception of the Object class from which everything is built.

The right-hand side window shows the actual code of whatever item we have selected. Unlike opening the file within a text file or our IDE, you will notice some hyperlinks located in the file. If you click on a hyperlink, it will take you to the associated class instantly so there is no need to look around for things.

For those who are programmers, or know how to read code, I would suggest starting out by looking at the `Actor`, `Object`, `Controller`, `Pawn`, and `Weapon` scripts as that will explain how a lot of things are done within the engine as per the gameplay. If not, don't worry as I will be explaining things as we go along.

There are a lot of other features within UnCodeX that are quite useful, but I leave that for you to explore; just know that as you get familiar with UnrealScript and write your own code, it will be quite a useful tool to bring into your workflow.

Sometimes when you're coding, you forget where that one specific variable is, or in general want to search if something may exist or not. While you can search for things in UnCodeX, it doesn't really make it obvious where something is, aside from what line it's on. Thankfully, there are tools that are there to help us with this exact problem.

Agent Ransack is a free file-searching utility that looks for things exactly as you type them, and will even show you exactly within the code where your stuff is located by making it bold and coloring it for you, making it quite easy to see. It is a free download at www.mythicsoft.com/agentransack/.

Setting up our IDE

There are two things required to use UnrealScript: source files and a compiler. UDK provides us with a way to compile the code, but we need some way to write code. Technically, all you need to create UnrealScript files for your project is a text editor of some sort, such as Notepad, and all of the code provided will work perfectly fine with it. However, programmers are inherently lazy, (otherwise we would still be writing in binary or assembly code) so over the years we have developed tools to make our lives easier. An Integrated Development Environment (IDE) is one such piece of software that provides a lot of functionality to make programming a much easier and more enjoyable experience.

If you happen to get a job with a company in the game industry that uses Unreal as their engine (as a licensee), you'll most likely be using nFringe (http://pixelminegames. com/nfringe/) and Visual Studio (http://www.microsoft.com/visualstudio/eng/downloads) as your choice of IDE, and while Visual Studio offers a free version, it is quite expensive to use nFringe for commercial projects, even for an Indie game license.

With that in mind, we will be using an open source UnrealScript IDE that is free for use and contains most of the functionality that the other IDEs provide.

Engage Thrusters

Let's get started and install the UnrealScript IDE!

1. First, go into the web browser of your choice and go to `http://uside.codeplex.com/`. From there, click on the purple **download** button.

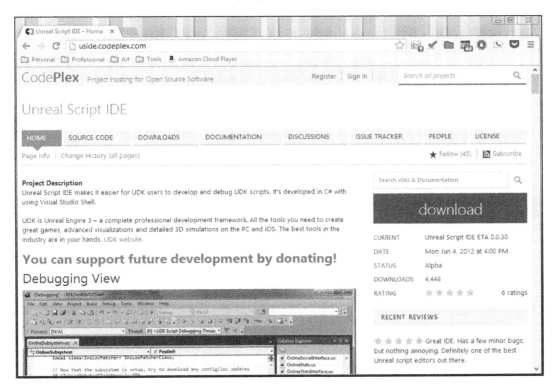

2. Once it has finished installing, double-click on the `UnrealScriptIDEInstall.exe` file in your `Downloads` folder.
3. Say **Yes** to the question asking if you want to install the UnrealScript IDE.

4. Next, you will see a question asking if you would like to install the Microsoft Visual Studio 2010 Shell (Isolated) Redistributable Package to which you will hit **Install** and wait for the download to finish.

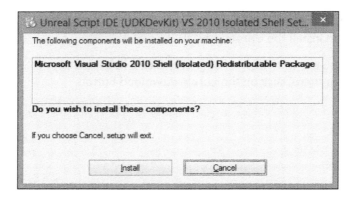

 It kind of goes without saying, but you should also have UDK installed prior to your installing of the UnrealScript IDE.

5. Once the download completes you will be brought to the Visual Studio 2010 shell download screen. Uncheck the **Yes, send information about my setup experiences to Microsoft Corporation** option if you like and then click the **Next** button.

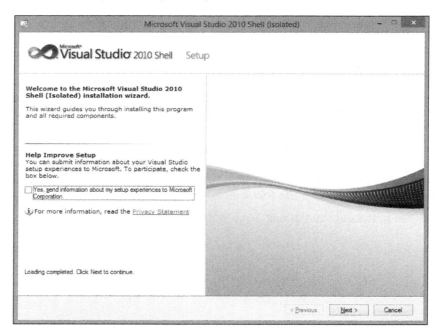

6. Accept the license agreement and select to install the full version of the program. When the installation completes, it will request for you to restart your computer. Do so.

7. With your computer restarted, double-click once again on the `UnrealScriptIDEInstall.exe` file to enter into the real installer.

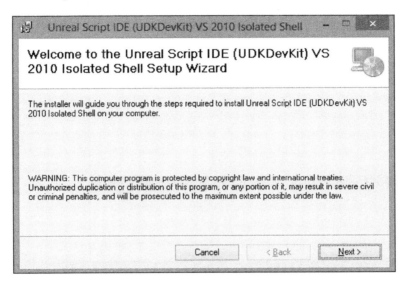

8. Follow the installer until you see the **Select UDK Binary Win32 Folder** section. At this point, make sure that you select the `Binaries\Win32` folder within your UDK installation path and then select **Next** and complete the installation.

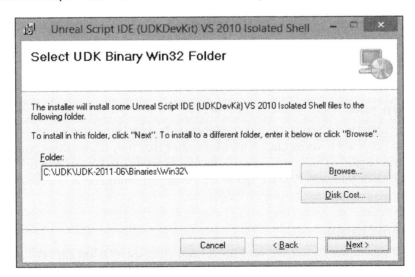

9. Now, go to your desktop and double-click on the UnrealScript IDE shortcut to start the program.

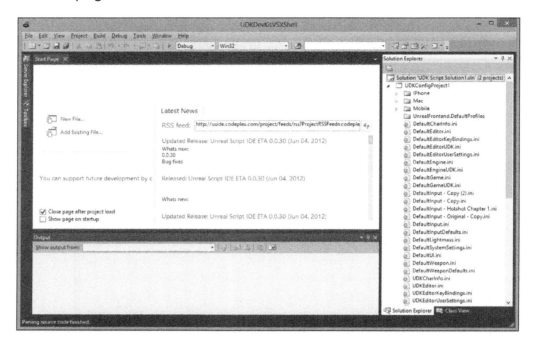

Objective Complete - Mini Debriefing

At this point, we have our IDE installed and ready to be used! It may look a bit complicated at first glance, but just like UDK, it is very powerful once we learn a bit about how it is used!

Classified Intel

Now, before we start coding, it is important to go over some fundamentals on coding.

The golden rule

When dealing with UnrealScript, the most important thing to remember is to *never directly alter any code provided to us by Epic*. A lot of the stuff that they have done connects to C++ code within the engine to have the game work, and may very well break the things that hold UDK together. All of the work that we will do and that you should do in the future should be from the files that we created.

Code commenting

When I formally sat down to learn how to code, I was stressed with the importance of creating clean code that is easy for someone to sit down and understand what is actually being done.

Commenting by using the /* and */ or // symbols removes whatever is written between the /* and */ symbols or the whole line with //. This can be very useful in terms of having a certain piece of code not get called, but the primary use of comments is telling things to people who may read your code (including your future self).

This way, if you have to come back to a piece of code down the road, you have some idea of what you were doing previously, or if you are asking for help on something you're writing, making your code as readable as possible will increase your chances of being helped, as finding the problem will be exceptionally easier.

You should *always* comment the code that you write. Programming, at its very core, is solving problems that have not been solved already. Code can only tell you *how* the program works; comments can tell you *why* it works.

That being said, it is possible to comment *too* much, or tell the reader something that is obvious or that can be understood easily. It is all about finding a balance.

Though this is about C/C++, the following article that describes how to go about commenting code is very good at explaining what is and what is not worth commenting:

`http://www.cprogramming.com/tutorial/comments.html`

"Hello world!" to UnrealScript

Now that we have all of the things required to write our code, it is time for us to write our first program! Since it was first written 40 years ago, it has been a tradition for novice programmers to write a function that displays "Hello world" on the screen. Let's do that now!

Engage Thrusters

Before we can write something to the screen though, we need to set up our packages so that Unreal will recognize what code we want to use in our project.

1. Back in the UnrealScript IDE, go to the **Solution Explorer** window on the right-hand side of the screen. Under the UDKConfigProject1 section, locate the DefaultEngine.ini file and double-click on it to open the file. Hit *Ctrl + F* to go to the Find window and search for [UnrealEd.EditorEngine]. When you get to that section, add the line +EditPackages=HotshotScripts after the last line of the +EditPackages section.

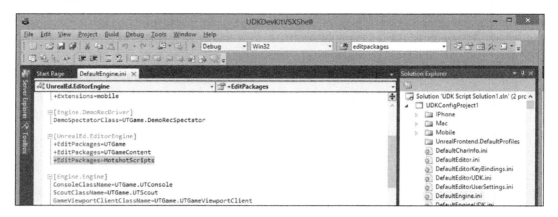

 You can use the Find window to search for things within a single file, or even all of the files within your two projects if you are trying to find something specific.

2. We are now done with `UDKConfigProject1`, so click on the down-pointing arrow on `UDKConfigProject1` in order to collapse it. Next, right-click on the `UDKSourceProject1` project and select **Add | New Folder**.

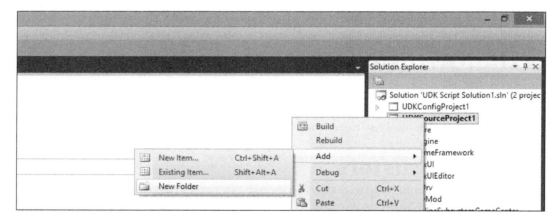

3. One you create the folder, you will see a new folder added with the name `NewFolder1`, which will be highlighted for you to change. Do so by giving it the name `HotshotScripts`.

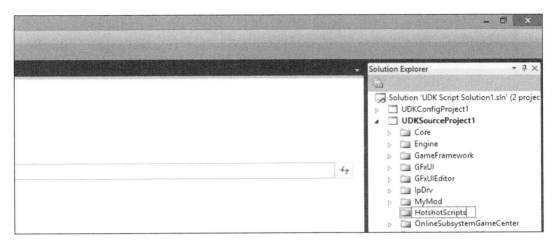

4. Right-click on the `HotshotScripts` folder and create another folder called `Classes`. After that, right-click once again on the folder and select **Add | New Item...**, and then in the window that pops up, under **Name** put `HelloWorldTrigger.uc`, then click on **Add**.

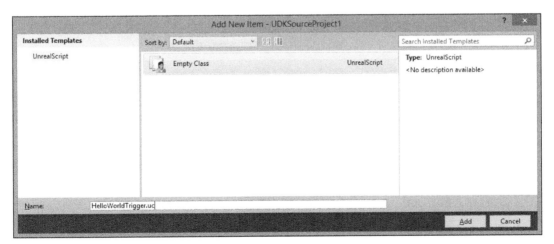

Once you add the file, you should now have a file structure that looks as shown in the following screenshot:

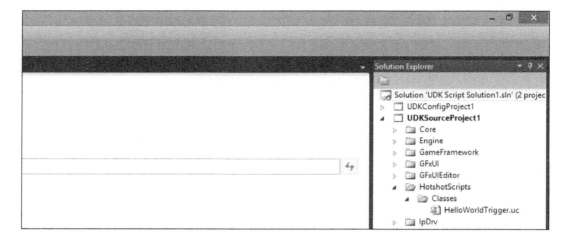

5. Now you should see on the left-hand side of the screen a tab with our new filename and some code included in it. Replace all of that code with the following:

```
// HelloWorldTrigger is a child of Trigger meaning it has
// all of the properties that a Trigger has.
// The placeable keyword means we can put it in the
// world.

class HelloWorldTrigger extends Trigger placeable;

// PostBeginPlay - Called whenever the level is loaded
//                 and play starts

function PostBeginPlay()
{
  // Calls the parent's (Trigger) function
  // with the same name
  super.PostBeginPlay();

  // Print "Hello world!" to the log window
  'log( "Hello World!");
}
```

This is depicted in the following screenshot:

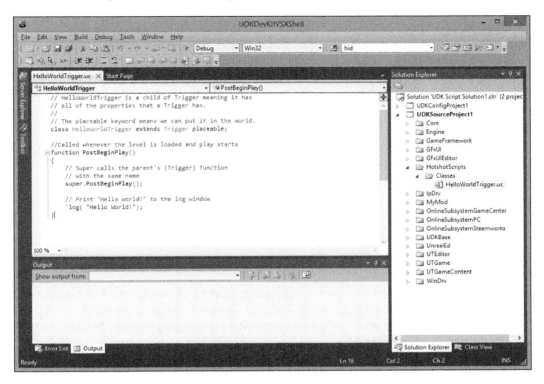

6. Now right-click on the `UDKSourceProject1` project and select **Properties**.

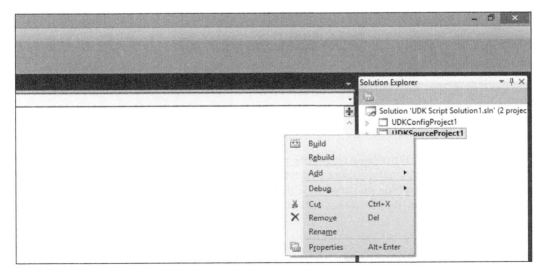

7. Under the Properties menu, add `editor` to the **Additional Command Line Arguments** section.

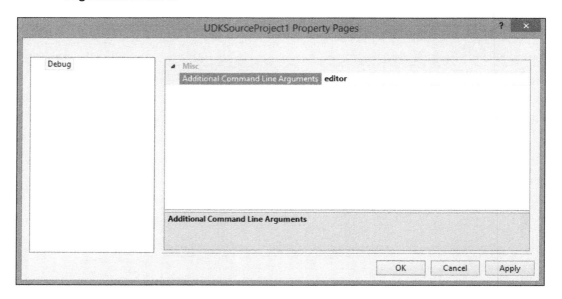

8. Start up the editor now by clicking on the **Start Debugging** button (the green arrow button) or by pressing *F5*.

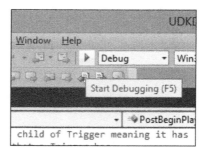

This will compile the newly created UnrealScript and open up UDK's editor for us.

This is the same as creating a shortcut for the UDK Editor with additional arguments. With this you can do things that are performed using the command line with the UDK executable. Note that `-log` does not work as the output is captured by the IDE in the **Output** tab.

9. At this point, UDK should be opened up. Now, inside the UDK editor go to the **Actor Classes** tab. At this point, if you extend the `Trigger` class, you will see our `HelloWorldTrigger` class.

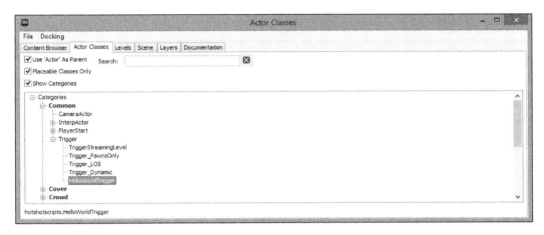

10. Click on the class within the **Actor Classes** tab and then go back to the editor. Within the default map, right-click and select **Add HelloWorldTrigger Here**. If you press *F4* to access the Properties window, confirm that it says **HelloWorldTrigger_0 Properties**.

11. I added a barrel to the level just for my confirmation that I was not within the default level. Do this if you wish.

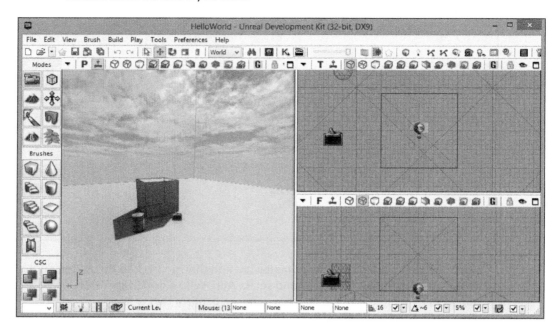

12. Now save the map as `HelloWorld.udk` within the `UDKGame\Content\Maps` folder and then exit out of UDK.

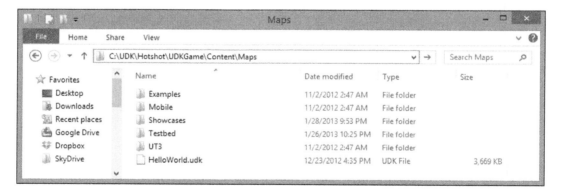

13. Now go to the UnrealScript IDE and access the Properties menu of the UDKSourceProject1 project once more. Under the Properties menu, add HelloWorld.udk -resX=800 -resY=600 -posY=-200 to the **Additional Command Line Arguments** option.

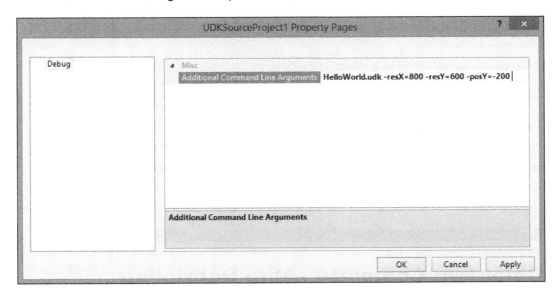

 In order for a map name to be passed as a command argument, it has to be somewhere within the UDKGame\Content\Maps folder or a folder within the Maps folder.

14. Start the program once again by either pressing *F4* or pressing the green arrow button that we used previously. Click on the green arrow again if the code pauses for a second. Now, once the game has started, on the bottom-right corner you should see a tab called **Output**. This holds the debug output as well as other information to be displayed every time when you use the 'log function. You'll notice this in the following script:

```
Log: LoadMap: HelloWorld.udk?Name=Player?Team=255
Log: Game class is 'SimpleGame'
Log: Primary PhysX scene will be in software.
Log: Creating Primary PhysX Scene.
Log: Bringing World HelloWorld.TheWorld up for play (0) at
2012.12.23-16.45.02
ScriptLog: Hello World!
Log: Bringing up level for play took: 0.008598
```

That our Hello World! was indeed called as we wanted it to!

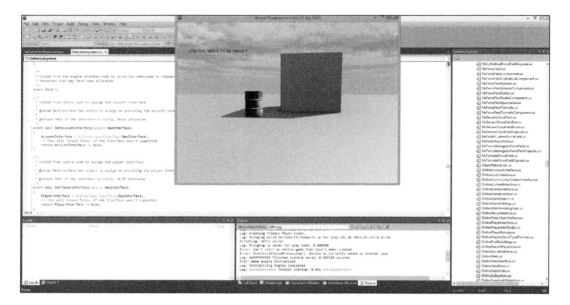

Objective Complete - Mini Debriefing

We have now written our very first program within UnrealScript and have a way of displaying the output information for ourselves. Though you may not think about it, we have also learned a lot on how working with UnrealScript works.

Creating a flickering light

Now that we have created something simple, let's attempt to create something a little less trivial.

Engage Thrusters

The following are the steps needed to create a light that flickers over time:

1. Open up our UnrealScript IDE again. Under the Properties menu, replace everything back to `editor` within the **Additional Command Line Arguments** option.

You can also just start up UDK and it will automatically ask you to recompile scripts if they have been changed.

2. Right-click on the `Hotshot\Classes` folder and select **Add | New Item...**, and then in the window that pops up under **Name** put `FlickeringLight.uc`, then click on **Add**.

3. Now replace the code provided with the following heavily commented code:

```
class FlickeringLight extends PointLightMovable placeable

//Removes Categories we don't need to see in the Editor
// HideCategories(Object, Debug, Advanced, Mobile,
                  Physics, Movement, Physics,Collision);

var(LightBrightness) float minBrightness;
var(LightBrightness) float maxBrightness;

var(Stability) float maxFlickerTime;
var(Stability) float maxStableTime;

var float timeToFlicker;
var float timeTilFlicker;

/*
ResetFlickerTime - Helper function that will reset
the light flickering variables to a new random number
*/

function ResetFlickerTime()
{
  //Change the light to be fully lit
  LightComponent.SetLightProperties(maxBrightness);

  // Pick a random number between 0 and the max time
  // fRand gives a random float between 0 and 1.
  timeTilFlicker = fRand() * maxStableTime;
  timeToFlicker = fRand() * maxFlickerTime;
}

// Called whenever the level is loaded and play starts
function PostBeginPlay()
{
  //Holds one of the variables if we need to switch them
```

```
    local float temp;

    // Super calls the parent's (Trigger) function
    // with the same name
    super.PostBeginPlay();

    // Do a bit of error checking
    if(maxBrightness < minBrightness)
    {
      temp=maxBrightness;
      maxBrightness=minBrightness;
      minBrightness= temp;
    }

    ResetFlickerTime();
}

// Tick - Called every frame within the game
event Tick(float DeltaTime)
{
  // local variable is only used within this function
  local float newBrightness;

  super.Tick(DeltaTime);

  // If it is time to flicker and there is still time to
  // flicker
  if((timeTilFlicker<=0)&&(timeToFlicker>0))
  {
    // find a random brightness from the lowest to the
    // highest possible
    newBrightness =minBrightness + (FRand() *
    (maxBrightness-minBrightness));
    // Then set our light to have this new brightness
    LightComponent.SetLightProperties(newBrightness);

    timeToFlicker -= DeltaTime;
  }
  // If that's not the case, let's see if we are done
  // flickering
  else if(timeToFlicker<=0)
  {
    ResetFlickerTime();
```

```
    }

    timeTilFlicker-=DeltaTime;
}

/* The defaultproperties section is where we initialize global
variables and what the editor will see them as when we add them by
default. */
defaultproperties
{
  minBrightness=0.0;
  maxBrightness=1.0;

  timeToFlicker=1.0;
  timeTilFlicker=3.0;

  maxFlickerTime=1.0;
  maxStableTime=3.0;
}
```

4. Save the file and start the game up again. Once the editor is up, go into the **Actor Classes** window and you will be able to find our FlickeringLight class.

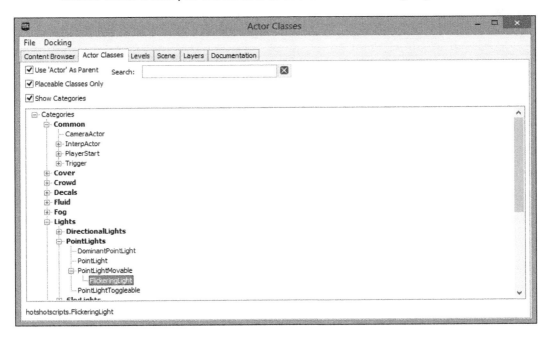

5. Now right-click on the level and select **Add FlickeringLight here**. If you open up the Properties tab, you will notice that most of the properties are no longer available except for the ones used by us. The reason this happens is due to the parentheses that I put around certain variables in the previous code. Those parentheses tell the editor that we wish to change those variables within the editor.

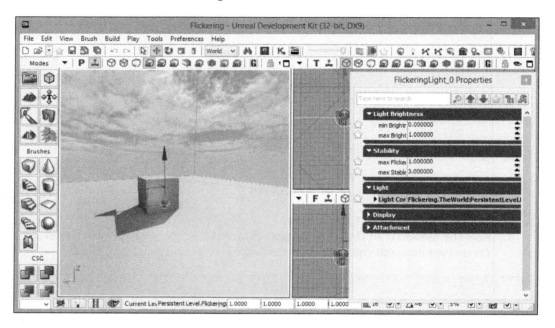

6. Create three flickering lights with the color of red, green, and blue and now click on each one of the lights in the editor, and play with their minimum and maximum brightness values to get them somewhere within the 0 - 10 range.

7. Save your project (by selecting **File | Save All**) `Flickering.udk`. Build your project by selecting **Build | Build All** and start your game by pressing *F8* or selecting **Play | In Editor** on the main toolbar.

Objective Complete - Mini Debriefing

Now it may not be too much to look at statically, but if you go in and play the level, you will notice that the light flickers for a period before being stable, and then flickers again! This can easily be extended in the previous projects we created by adding additional touches of color, which can make the environments much more colorful and dynamic, such as the projects we created in *Project 3, Terror in Deep Space*, and *Project 4, Terror in Deep Space 2: Even Deeper*.

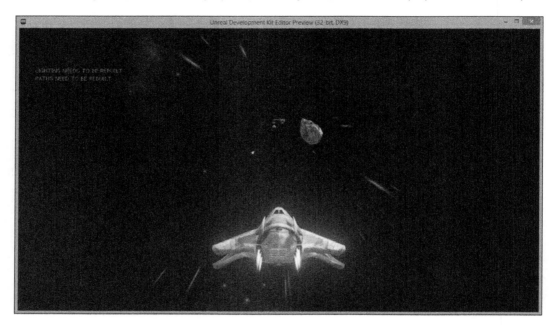

Mission Accomplished

With this project, we should have acquired a fundamental understanding of how powerful UnrealScript can be, and a hint at what can be done with it, as well as a glance at tools that will make our lives much easier as UnrealScript developers. Let's take one final look at our project:

Classified Intel

For those wishing to learn more about UnrealScript, here are some additional web pages that I recommend you to check out:

- The Unreal Developer's Network has a complete section on their website devoted to UnrealScript at `http://udn.epicgames.com/Three/UnrealScriptHome.html`.

- Also on UDN, this is a great primer on creating UnrealScript and when to use certain parameters and what they mean. In particular, *Chapter 3, Classes in Unreal* is recommended for reading; it can be found at `http://udn.epicgames.com/Three/MasteringUnrealScriptClasses.html`.

- Once you feel confident enough, check out the UnrealScript Reference on UDK. It assumes that the reader has a working knowledge of C/C++, and is familiar with object-oriented programming. It also assumes that the reader has played with Unreal and used the UnrealEd editing environment. The reference is located at `http://udn.epicgames.com/Three/UnrealScriptReference.html`.

- Some frequently asked questions about coding in UnrealScript can be found at `http://wiki.beyondunreal.com/Legacy:Unreal_Coding_FAQ`.

- And for those having more specific questions, Epic Games has a fairly large community that can be found at `http://forums.epicgames.com/forums/367-UDK-Programming-and-Unrealscript`.

You Ready to go Gung HO? A Hotshot Challenge

Through this project, we have learned how to create our own functionality in UDK through UnrealScript within a short period of time, but there are still plenty of things we can do! How about you take some time between projects and try to complete the following:

▸ Create your own version of the `Actor` class that you most frequently use, and hide the categories that you don't use

▸ Change the asteroid that we created in the rail-shooter project into a class, converting the behavior we created in Kismet in UnrealScript

▸ Replace the player's default SkeletalMesh to one of your own choice

▸ Modify one of the weapons so that it does not need ammo to fire

▸ Learn how to create your own custom Kismet action

▸ Learn more about UnrealScript and create new games of your own

Index

Thank you for buying
Mastering UDK Game Development HOTSHOT

About Packt Publishing

Packt, pronounced 'packed', published its first book "*Mastering phpMyAdmin for Effective MySQL Management*" in April 2004 and subsequently continued to specialize in publishing highly focused books on specific technologies and solutions.

Our books and publications share the experiences of your fellow IT professionals in adapting and customizing today's systems, applications, and frameworks. Our solution based books give you the knowledge and power to customize the software and technologies you're using to get the job done. Packt books are more specific and less general than the IT books you have seen in the past. Our unique business model allows us to bring you more focused information, giving you more of what you need to know, and less of what you don't.

Packt is a modern, yet unique publishing company, which focuses on producing quality, cutting-edge books for communities of developers, administrators, and newbies alike. For more information, please visit our website: www.packtpub.com.

Writing for Packt

We welcome all inquiries from people who are interested in authoring. Book proposals should be sent to author@packtpub.com. If your book idea is still at an early stage and you would like to discuss it first before writing a formal book proposal, contact us; one of our commissioning editors will get in touch with you.

We're not just looking for published authors; if you have strong technical skills but no writing experience, our experienced editors can help you develop a writing career, or simply get some additional reward for your expertise.

UnrealScript Game Programming Cookbook

ISBN: 978-1-84969-556-5   Paperback: 272 pages

Discover how you can augment your game development with the power of UnrealScript

1. Create a truly unique experience within UDK using a series of powerful recipes to augment your content

2. Discover how you can utilize the advanced functionality offered by the Unreal Engine with UnrealScript

3. Learn how to harness the built-in AI in UDK to its full potential

Grome Terrain Modeling with Ogre3D, UDK, and Unity3D

ISBN: 978-1-84969-939-6   Paperback: 162 pages

Create massive terrains and export them to the most popular game engines

1. A comprehensive guide for terrain creation

2. Step-by-step walkthrough of Grome 3.1 and toolset

3. Export terrains to Unity3D, UDK, and Ogre3D

Please check **www.PacktPub.com** for information on our titles

Unreal Development Kit Game Design Cookbook

ISBN: 978-1-84969-180-2   Paperback: 544 pages

Over 100 recipes to accelerate the process of learning game design with UDK

1. An intermediate, fast-paced UDK guide for game artists

2. The quickest way to face the challenges of game design with UDK

3. All the necessary steps to get your artwork up and running in game

4. Part of Packt's Cookbook series: Each recipe is a carefully organized sequence of instructions to complete the task as efficiently as possible

UDK iOS Game Development Beginner's Guide

ISBN: 978-1-84969-190-1   Paperback: 280 pages

Create your own third-person shooter game using the Unreal Development Kit to create your own game on Apple's iOS devices, such as the iPhone, iPad, and iPod Touch

1. Learn the fundamentals of the Unreal Editor to create gameplay environments and interactive elements

2. Create a third person shooter intended for the iOS and optimize any game with special considerations for the target platform

3. Take your completed game to Apple's App Store with a detailed walkthrough on how to do it

Please check **www.PacktPub.com** for information on our titles

Lightning Source UK Ltd.
Milton Keynes UK
UKOW05f0120150815

256945UK00010B/91/P